GROWING UP SOUTHERN

Fred Brown and Jeanne McDonald

Growing Up Southern
How the South shapes its writers

ISBN 1 889893 13 7

Published by
Emerald House Group, Inc.
Blue Ridge Publishing
1 Chick Springs Road, Suite 206
Greenville, SC 29609 USA

and

Ambassador Productions
16 Hillview Avenue
Belfast, Northern Ireland
BT5 6JH

ACKNOWLEDGMENTS

With grateful appreciation to the Tennessee Arts Commission for past
support, to Willie Morris for suggestions and inspiration, and to the
Mississippi Department of Archives and History.

For our mothers

Carolyn Pratts
and
Jane Williams Brown (1912-1958)

Contents

Preface

This book is the result of a dinner conversation that ended with the question, "How are southern writers different from other writers?"

We determined to find out for ourselves, and in the resulting interviews with writers who grew up in the South, we began to discover common denominators that shaped their childhoods, and subsequently, their work.

All of the authors we chose were born in the first half of this century and thus have lived through vast social and technological change. Though a few came from relatively privileged backgrounds, many were reared in humble rural or agricultural settings, but all lived in fairly insulated, and sometimes isolated, communities. In almost every instance, we can recognize in these writers what T.S. Eliot called a voice that reflects "ancestral traits" evolving from a strong sense of history.

It has always been challenging to define southern literature, and although there is a long list of basic elements that set it apart from other regional writing, it seems simpler to say, "You know it when you see it."

Throughout all our lively and fulfilling conversations with these writers, we found humor, warmth, intelligence, and a huge helping of southern graciousness and hospitality. Our only regret has been that during the time we did these interviews, Eudora Welty was too frail to meet with us. But thanks to her own autobiography and information supplied to us by Willie Morris, we were able to include her profiles. In many other ways, her presence is felt throughout this book because so many writers we talked to have paid tribute to her inestimable contribution to southern literature.

In these pages you can see for yourself that modern southern literature is still energetic, electric, and diversified. Not only that, the indications are that it also has a promising future with the emerging generation of writers who have grown up in the New South. It is reassuring to know that there will always be a voice out there with a decidedly southern accent.

You'll know it when you hear it.

Fred Brown and Jeanne McDonald

Mike Curtis second row, third from the left. The Darkroom. Photo courtesy of Mike Curtis.

Introduction

The generating experiences shared by the writers portrayed in this book are surprisingly numerous: gifted teachers; an intense level of family piety; a startling, even traumatic, discovery of persistent racial inequality; a troubled or handicapped family member; high and early ambition; and a growing awareness of regional history, in particular the emotional residue of a war their grandparents had fought and sometimes survived but, inescapably, lost.

Just how the broad shadow of that terrible war, fought to defend the right of southern states to decide their own destinies and to preserve their "peculiar institution," should lead a generation of the South's best and brightest toward a commitment to racial justice and amity is not altogether clear. But virtually all of these writers report a childhood acceptance of the status quo— which is to say, in most cases, a rigid segregation of schools, churches, most public and a great many private enterprises—followed by a period of dismay and then growing egalitarian resolve.

Being a "southern" writer, however, has to do with more than a convulsive turnabout on the question of racial equality and opportunity. Most of the writers describe growing up with a powerful sense of community, usually small town community, with an agricultural economy, vigorous church life, shared values, and a strong sense of history's hold on family tradition and expectations.

Richard Marius, for example, grew up on a small farm near Lenoir City, Tennessee. He studied first at his state university, then in Paris, briefly at a New Orleans seminary, and finally at Yale, before embarking on a teaching and writing career capped by a long stint as director of Harvard's required undergraduate courses in Expository Writing. For Marius, a consuming sense of history distinguished southern writing from work produced elsewhere. "The southern writer," he says, "nearly always writes about the past, especially the kind of southern writer who is now dying off." That past, in Marius' view, is not wholly comforting to writers, who, while dependent upon its themes and rhythms, are simultaneously alienated from its sometimes anti-rational biases and backward-looking obstinacies.

Like Marius, Elizabeth Spencer grew up with a Bible never far from her hand. As a child in Carrollton, Mississippi, she attended church and Sunday school four times on Sunday, and went to Wednesday night prayer meeting. Even summer camp was church-related, and Bellhaven College, a girls' school in Jackson, Mississippi, which Spencer attended in the 1930's, "might as well have been a convent."

The impact of this force-feeding of a lively and intelligent young woman was predictable. While religious themes surface repeatedly in Spencer's work, they are accompanied by a quiet protest against the rigidity and organizational zeal of the institutional church. One critic of Spencer's writing insists that her "consistent concern with the tyrannies of community" make her a distinctly 'southern' writer. No matter where a Spencer story is set, says Terry Roberts in a book published in 1994 by LSU Press, "its primary concern is that quintessentially southern one—the individual caught in the communal web."

Tension between the individual and the entrapments of "community" also figure in Doris Betts' fiction. Like so many other writers in this book, Betts started life on the outskirts of small town life, in her case on a farm outside of Statesville, North Carolina, in a house with no running water, no electricity, and no telephone. A respect for literature, however, induced Betts' parents to make possible a college education for their daughter, who has included them, thinly disguised, in several of her stories.

In Betts' view, a transformation is taking place in southern fiction, having chiefly to do with the distance in years and generations between the Civil War and the concern of southern young people. "Stories of the Civil War," she says, "have transmuted to more individual history and family history, county history, local history. . . . As a southern preoccupation it is pretty well gone now, at least among my students."

Shifts in class origin offer another source of transformation, Betts argues. "These days you don't have aristocratic plantation writers, like Faulkner. You have people who have come out of beauty shops and trailer parks— plebeian middle class and lower class writers who never went to war and are not that much interested in traditions of glory and valor." Moreover, Betts muses, "the land of cotton is the integrated, urbanized, crowded land of the computer. In the Kmart checkout line, Dilsey's descendants and those from the Compson and Sartoris clans are all wearing jeans."

Lee Smith agrees: "I might have a student who has grown up at the mall in Fayetteville and her parents have split up and she's lived a lot of places, but she writes a story which, though it doesn't take place in a small town, still has a voice that is thoroughly southern."

One emerging southern writer portrayed in this book did go to war, and he did not grow into adulthood innocently accepting of antebellum traditions. He is Yusef Komunyakaa, a black poet born in Bogalusa, Louisiana, and 1994 winner of the Pulitzer Prize for poetry. Not surprisingly, his themes are less wedded to the crumbling of plantation aristocracy than to the gritty realities of family and economic survival in the New South, and to the moral ambiguities of a war fought for national honor, but understood, often to the consternation of veterans like Komunyakaa, as an occasion of national disgrace.

Like others in this volume, Komunyakaa was drawn early and obsessively into books, any books that opened up to him a larger, more complicated world. Among them, characteristically, was the Bible, which he read straight through and then began to read again, until startled by the dawning realization that the churches he knew were segregated. No whites came to worship at his church, and no blacks attended the town's white church. The contradiction shook his faith in biblical inerrancy, but it also led him to an exercise in logic and eventually to a reflective stance that admires "a kind of spirituality in people who try to be decent and good." Religiosity per se, he felt forced to conclude, was not identical with goodness. In much the same way, Komunyakaa grew up tightly wedded to community, but to the community that stood always at the end of the line and performed the janitorial function for a larger whiter community of the whole.

No wonder that, for Komunyakaa, the themes he is drawn to again and again involve "seeing beauty in a place and terror at the same time. It goes back to the ritual observed in nature as a child. You see beauty and terror side by side. That is what poetry is made of, beauty and terror.

The alignment that tracks a certain kind of tension."

That tension, as Elizabeth Cox points out, has made the South ripe for storytelling. Shelby Foote admits that the persecuted class who fell victims to the tension also created the social layers that have supplied the necessary element of conflict to the classic southern story. "Imagine a Russian novel without peasants in it," he says. "A writer can place a value on terrible, terrible things. With the South and slavery, you had a society that was stacked up in different parts. That makes you conscious of your relationships with other people and what happens when their rules are crossed or broken. Without those levels, you have no grounds for moral indignation any more."

Most of the writers in this collection, most notably, Eudora Welty, remember happy and insulated childhoods, though none was without its occasional bumps. Although their economic circumstances were different, Willie Morris, Allen Wier and George Garrett found pleasure in the uncomplicated pleasures of boyhood. Fred Chappell agrees with Graham Greene that "childhood is a writer's capital." And nearly all of these writers had close relationships with aunts, uncles or grandparents. Others, like Komunyakaa, Elizabeth Spencer and Jayne Anne Phillips, dreamed themselves away to other places and eventually traveled far but remained in the South emotionally.

My interest in the   question—What is a southern writer?—stems from the portion of my own childhood spent in Hardy (population, 504), a rural hamlet nestled in the foothills of northeastern Arkansas. I lived in Hardy for the better part of five years before traveling south to Magnolia, Arkansas, for a final year in high school. In those years (the late 1940's), Hardy was largely isolated.

No paved highways in or out of town, and buses or trains that appeared only irregularly. A few Hardy homes had electric lighting or plumbing, but central heating was unheard of.

During those years, I lived with Henry and Miriam Norman, a couple in their sixties who represented the best of what Hardy had to offer.

Hank, as he was universally known, ran a lumber yard and played on the town baseball team until well into his sixties. He was laconic, plain-spoken, all business, and not a man of great warmth or cultural interests. He was, however, widely respected for his firmness, his fundamental decency, and for his willingness, if necessary, to support his convictions with his fists. Miriam was from an old Memphis family. She owned one of Hardy's few pianos, belonged to the Book-of-the-Month Club, and tried her best to bring civility and broad interests into the life of the stony adolescent (me) for whom she'd agreed to provide foster care.

I'd come to Hardy from a succession of private progressive schools in the North, and I had convinced each of them that my problems were all but untreatable, perhaps unknowable, and that I would be better off in a school or social environment administered by men with guns.

The Normans did not fit that description, of course, and Hardy represented a radical shift from Manhattan and its environs. But Hardy had a library, a Methodist church, at least a couple of outdoor basketball courts, and, unmistakably, a sense of community. It was precisely what I needed, and my years there were, on the whole, as happy and restorative as I would let them be.

Unlike so many of the writers in this book, I did not have inspired or particularly encouraging teachers, and the Hardy town library was not the sort of resource likely to invite or strengthen a love of literature. Its adult book collection featured mainly western novels by the likes of Max Brand and Ernest Haycox, or mysteries by Ellery Queen and Erle Stanley Gardner. But it was there that I discovered the novels of Pearl Buck and, in spite of the vigorous opposition of the town librarian, raced through *The Good Earth* and *Dragon Seed* without obvious harm.

If the Normans had a Bible, I wasn't aware of it. Religious worship, in any case, was not an obvious component of their domestic routine. I irregularly attended Sunday School at Hardy's Methodist Church, though mainly because the class included so many of the high school's prettiest young women. The biblicism I encountered there was deeply felt, but not very reflective, and I fairly quickly outwore my welcome by asking questions, usually having to do with literalism, that the helpless volunteers responsible for our instruction were not well prepared to answer. In time, I fell away, and did not open a Bible again for more than 30 years, when special family circumstances argued for re-entry—and, of course, brought me face to face with one of the principal taproots of Western culture.

Hardy's uncomplicatedness, its isolation from the post-war shiftings and reconfigurations occurring all around it, were also its charm and its strength, at least to a boy who needed mainly to be left alone, to be allowed to find his way slowly back into the world. I spent my time reading, stalking imaginary Cherokees in the cornfields that spread around the Norman homestead, and reflecting on my state of exile. I came to enjoy the mile-long walk along the Spring River into town, the idea that meals might consist of what was growing in your garden and what you'd been feeding or gathering in your hen-house. Hank Norman's durable silences left me little to object to, and Miriam Norman taught me card games and even, briefly, the piano. She encouraged me to range freely through her small library, and only once—when Hardy's school superintendent let her know that my acid and vocal assessment of a high school English teacher had driven the poor woman to the brink of resignation—did she ask me to think hard about my effect on the people around me.

On political matters we agreed, simply, to disagree. Hardy, like most of Northeastern Arkansas, had a homogeneous population: all white, with vaguely Scotch-Irish-English roots, virtually all Protestant, and without sharp class distinctions, though an uncomfortable number of families lived lives of grinding poverty. No black person lived within 100 miles, and Jews and Catholics, though occasionally referred to on the schoolyard, were essentially unknown, and therefore much maligned. Harry Truman was challenging the rights of states to insist on segregation in the face of growing pressure from the federal government and courts to initiate the polar shift that enveloped America a few years later. The Normans, though unlikely to be affected by these changes, were nonetheless resolute in opposing them. My views were quite different, and after a few tart exchanges, we silently agreed to talk of other things. My schoolmates were not so kind, or so forgiving, but they too could see the futility of perpetual discord.

In this respect, my experiences differ markedly from those of most writers in this book. Coming from the radicalized sector of an already high-minded North, I was trouble waiting to happen. When in Little Rock, I moved to rear seats of transit buses, thus enraging black passengers, for whom those seats were reserved, and white passengers, who wanted no crusades. And I would let no racial remark, benign or mischievous, pass through Hardy's classrooms without challenge.

When not laying the groundwork for my own private Appomattox, I lived the life of other Hardy boys, worrying mostly about our basketball teams, playing pool at the Green Rabbit Cafe, swimming in the Spring River, or listening to St. Louis Cardinal baseball games at Padgett's Service Station. I'd never lived life so simply, nor so safely. I was sorry to leave, though I certainly had to.

Many of the writers in this book left towns the size of Hardy, or even smaller, and have traveled widely in search of a worldly education and professional opportunity. Significantly, none of them has ever been able—or wanted—to leave behind the shadings, the night sounds, the vivid speech or emotional terrain they explored as children. Perhaps, as Thomas Wolfe so sagely declared, you can't go home again. On the other hand, who among us has ever truly left?

C. Michael Curtis

Photo by Martin Cornel.

The Authors

Photograph courtesy of Shelby Foote.

SHELBY FOOTE

"If southerners talk a lot about the Civil War, that's easy to account for. When I was coming along, if you had a difference of opinion with another boy, you had a fistfight. The ones I remember with the greatest clarity are the ones I lost. And that is the way it is with the Civil War."

Just off a busy street in midtown Memphis, Shelby Foote's grand old Tudor house sits cloistered behind a brick-walled garden of tangled vines and flowering shrubs. To enter that secret place is to be transported to an old southern setting, one that might have been created by Faulkner, or, for that matter, by Shelby Foote himself.

As you step through the garden gate that swings inward from the driveway, a casement window opens from the second floor of the house, and Shelby Foote leans out. "Good morning," he says. "I'll be right down." He speaks in the mellifluous voice that has become familiar to countless Americans through his narration of Ken Burns' Civil War television series, his speech blurred by the soft, fluid accent of his youth in Greenville, Mississippi.

You can't help thinking how the overgrown garden creates the perfect sense of place so essential to Foote:

the stilled fountain, its basin green with a mossy patina, the stone steps weathered with silvery lichen. When you comment on the wild beauty of the garden, he apologizes. It is presently unkempt, he explains, because the gardener has "disappeared."

Surely, though, you exclaim, he will be back.

"I don't think so," Foote says placidly. "I believe he shot a man."

Here are the basic elements of the classic southern story—errant gardener, alleged violence, the overgrown garden, unyielding humidity, and the narrator's calm acceptance of the way things are. It's the perfect introduction to one of the South's most famous writers.

Shelby Foote is the quintessential southern gentleman. His regal bearing and thick silver hair and beard give him a presence that demands respect, though he looks much younger than his biography claims him to be. In private he is gracious and warm, with a highly infectious laugh that puts visitors immediately at ease, while his public persona is often aloof, even forbidding, perhaps to protect him from the national celebrity gained from the Civil War series. His candor is abrupt, sometimes blistering, but Foote is a stickler for the truth, in his writing as well as in his personal relationships. For his three-volume Civil War narrative, he painstakingly researched and documented every conversation, every piece of correspondence, every battle strategy, to make each event reflect the actual circumstances. The craft of storytelling, he declares, may be even more important for the historian than for the novelist, and plotting more important in history than in fiction.

If Shelby Foote is now famous, his fame is well deserved. And if, as he says, sales of his books have "shot over the moon" since the Ken Burns series aired, all the better. It is rare that a writer of history has a chance to become a commercial success, but in this case, both Foote and the public have benefitted.

Foote has been called stubborn, distant, spoiled, and self-centered, all of which serve only to make him a more interesting and enigmatic figure. He is also gracious, humorous, and brilliant. The television series is only part of the general aura that surrounds his life. Even his personal history is romantic. His father was the son of a wealthy Mississippi planter, who, shortly after his son married Foote's mother, gambled away the entire family business. As Foote phrases it, he "pushed the plantation across the poker table." Through the intervention of his father-in-law, the elder Foote became a shipping clerk at Armour Company in Greenville, and within six years he was manager of all the company's southern operations.

Shelby Foote was born on November 17, 1916, in Greenville. During his childhood the family moved from place to place—Mobile, Vicksburg, and Pensacola. In September of 1922, when Shelby was five years old, his father died, and he and his mother returned to Greenville to live with his aunt and uncle.

"It is very hard for me to say how my father's death affected me," says Foote now. "I don't remember any traumatic reaction to it. I do remember one reaction that is not without its humor. A shipping clerk who had worked closely with my father was assigned the task of telling me the bad news. He took me outside and we sat in one of those swings that sits in a frame, facing each other. He said, 'Shelby Junior, your daddy's gone away, and I'm sorry to have to tell you that.'

"I said, 'You mean he died?' Mr. Watts was embarrassed. 'Yes,' he said. I remember feeling a terrific sense of responsibility because I was the survivor, you see. Then I said the thing that really knocked Mr. Watts out of the swing. I said, 'Who will get his money?'

That question was an early indication of Shelby Foote's no-nonsense approach to life. " I was an only child," he says, "and with my father dead, I got two enormous benefits. One was that I was often left to my own resources, so I became a reader. The other was, that at the rate my father was being promoted in Armour Company, I almost surely would have wound up in Oak Park, Illinois, instead of Mississippi, and I would have been a Chicagoan.

"I'm sorry my daddy had to die to save me from that, but I am glad to be saved from it. I'm sure there was trauma when he died, and looking back on it, I must have felt that he had deserted us somehow.

"My mother did not appear or act strong, but she was. After Daddy died and we came back to Greenville, she and two other women opened a little gift shop, selling embroidered handkerchiefs and things like that. She also began to study shorthand. Then, when I was entering the fourth grade, she got a job with Armour in Pensacola, where my daddy had been manager. So we moved to Pensacola for three or four years and then came back to Greenville when my mother's father died."

When the Footes returned to Greenville, Shelby entered the seventh grade. Later he was appointed editor of *The Pica* (named for a bird, not a printing measurement), which, under his hand, earned the reputation of being the best high school newspaper in the country. Walker Percy, Foote's lifelong friend, was the paper's gossip columnist.

Foote's high school career stretched to five years because he paid no attention to the requirements for earning his diploma. "I just took what I wanted to take and didn't take what I didn't want to take and when it came time to graduate with the rest of the people in my class I didn't have enough credits to graduate, so I had to stay another year. That was good, because Walker had been a year ahead of me, and his brother Leroy and I were in the same class."

The friendship of Foote and Walker Percy has recently been documented in a collection of their letters edited by Jay Tolson (*The Correspondence of Shelby Foote and Walker Percy,* Doubletake/Norton, New York, 1997). The two met as teenagers one day when Walker introduced himself to the thirteen-year-old Foote in the Greenville Country Club swimming pool. The Percy boys and their mother had gone to live with their uncle Will Percy in Greenville after the suicide of their father the summer before. Foote was delighted to meet Walker because Will Percy's house was a gathering place for poets, journalists, novelists, and other celebrities. But Foote gained much more that afternoon than the promise of an exciting summer. What grew from that acquaintance was a solid, unshakeable friendship that lasted 60 years and ended only with Walker Percy's death in 1990.

The two boys were alike in many ways. Both were witty and independent, irreverent and cynical. "We were as bad as any boys anywhere I know of," says Foote, without the slightest trace of apology. "We did terrible things, including shoplifting. But there was something about relationships between people in those days that was different."

Percy once said he had been responsible for Foote's becoming a writer. "As a matter of fact, it was Walker's and my friendship with each other that led us to do some very advanced reading for kids," Foote says. "I remember in 1934, I guess it was, I was a sophomore or junior in high school. I heard somewhere, probably from Mr. Will, that the three big novels of the 20th century so far were probably Joyce's *Ulysses,* Proust's *Remembrance of Things Past* and Thomas Mann's *Magic Mountain.* So that summer I read all three of those books. That is the kind of reading we did." The influence of Proust was so powerful, that to this day, Foote keeps his portrait hanging beside his desk.

Foote had done some prodigious reading for his age before that, however. "The first modern novel I ever read was about 1932. Faulkner's *Light in August* had just come out. That is a helluva first novel to read. It practically knocked me off my feet. Here was somebody writing about my homeland and enabling me to see it better than I had ever seen it before."

Even before that, when he was ten or eleven years old, he was given a copy of *David Copperfield* in a Sunday School class. "I had read all kinds of stuff, *Tom Swift* and that sort of thing, but when I finished *David Copperfield,* I knew David better than I knew anybody, including myself. Here was a whole world sitting there waiting for me. I didn't then sit down and read all of Dickens. I let it percolate slowly. But right then I knew there was something worth waiting for."

His reading choices were not always received positively, however. Foote incensed his high school principal when he was discovered reading *Ulysses* in the school newspaper room when he should have been in physical education class. It was the last straw for the principal, who, weary of Foote's insubordination, sent a letter to the University of North Carolina at Chapel Hill, where Foote had applied for admission, urging them not to accept him as a student. But on registration day Foote appeared at the registrar's office and talked his way in anyway.

Despite the principal's reaction, Foote remembers high school as "fun." One teacher in particular inspired him. "Everybody has had a wonderful teacher at some point. Mine was L.E. Hawkins. She made, I think, $125 a month. She was an old maid. And she was wonderful. She didn't know all that much Shakespeare, but she managed to communicate to me her love for his work. I remember once when grades were coming out, she said, 'Now Shelby, you made a B, but you should have made an A, so I'm giving you a C.'"

In Walker Percy, Foote had found a friend his age who loved reading as much as he. That first summer began a running argument between the two. "Walker was a Tolstoy fan and I was a Dostoevsky fan. I kept claiming that Tolstoy was the greatest slick writer who ever lived. About 35 or 40 years later Walker and I were driving across Lake Pontchartrain and he suddenly said, 'You know, Shelby, you were right on that.'

"If it had not been for Walker, yes, I might not have been a writer. But I can also say if it hadn't been for me, he wouldn't have been a writer. Walker was like Conrad. His first novel didn't come out until he was past 40. In our letters, it sounds like I'm up on a podium as God Almighty talking to a neophyte. What I was trying to do was warn him about the dangers I had learned through writing five novels. I was two years into the Civil War before Walker's first novel was published. Through all this, we were each other's best friends. That's not only unusual, but for two writers, it is unheard of. There was never any competition between us."

As boys growing up in the Mississippi Delta, the two were busy having fun. "We went to lots of dances. We were all dancing fools. One Christmas holiday I went to 12 dances in 10 days, including two tea dances. Greenville was a great place to grow up. There weren't many social barriers. One of your best friends might be the son of president of the bank and your other best friend might be the son of a fireman. The town was about 15,000 then. And that meant, for nine months out of the year, five or so hours a day, every white child in that town, male and female, was in that same high school studying. You got to know each other during those extremely impressionistic years in a way that I don't think anybody does anymore. Very few people left town and very few people came to town, so people were close. A contributing factor was that this was in the Depression, when there wasn't any question of kids going off to prep school. People had barely enough money to put shoes on their feet, let alone provide tuition to some prep school."

There were other far more exciting things to think about. One was the day that Shelby Foote walked up and knocked on William Faulkner's door. "Walker and I were going up to Sewanee in East Tennessee. The way we were going led us more or less through Oxford. We were about 20 years old, either just out of school or just fixing to be out. He was in medical school and I had left Chapel Hill. I said, 'We ought to stop by and see William Faulkner, he's in Oxford.' Walker said, 'I don't know that man well enough to knock on his door.' I said, 'Hell, he's a writer, it's all right.' After all, he'd been knocking at my door with all those books, so why shouldn't I knock on his door?

"We got there and drove in the Rowan Oak driveway. They used to have a big Keep Out: No Trespassing sign on it. I parked the car and Walker wouldn't get out.

"So I went up and knocked and Faulkner opened the door. I said, 'Mr. Faulkner, my name is Shelby Foote, I'm from Greenville. That's Will Percy's adopted son out there in the car and I want to know from you where I can find a copy of *The Marble Faun*.' I didn't want a copy, of course. I just wanted to talk to Faulkner.

"He said, 'Well, I don't have one, but you might talk to my agent, Leland Hayward. He could find one for you maybe.' I said, 'Fine.' Then he said, 'Come on and walk out here with me,' and we walked down the line of cedar trees.

"Faulkner said, 'You're from over in the Delta, aren't you? I just finished a book about your country this morning.' I asked him what it was called. He said, 'It's called *If I Forget Thee, Jerusalem*.' I didn't know what to make of that.

"We talked a while longer about the Delta. Then as we were going toward the house, Walker was still in the car and I introduced him. Faulkner acknowledged him and went into the house and we drove on off.

"I kept waiting for *If I Forget Thee, Jerusalem* to come out and it didn't. About six months later, a book called *The Wild Palms* came out. It wasn't until about five or six years ago that I learned from Joseph Blotner's Faulkner biography that the original title of *Wild Palms* was *If I Forget Thee, Jerusalem*. So, he really had finished it that morning we met.

"Walker was sorry forever afterwards, but it was just like Walker not to do that."

Years later, Foote went with Ben Wasson to have dinner with Faulkner and his wife Estelle. "Ben lived in Greenville and he did the rewrite on Faulkner's *Flags in the Dust,* retitled *Sartoris.* He shortened it so it could be published by Harcourt-Brace. He and Faulkner were good friends, so he carried me over there for dinner. That was the first time I had spent any time talking with Faulkner sure enough. Then he came to Greenville when *Notes on a Horse Thief* came out. He showed some interest in *Shiloh,* so when it was published the next year I sent him a copy.

"His stepson, Malcolm, said Faulkner told him Shiloh was a better novel than *The Red Badge of Courage.* High praise, isn't it? Later another friend said Faulkner told him how much he admired my book, and the friend said, 'Bill, you ought to write Shelby Foote a note and tell him that. It would give him great pleasure to hear that from you.' And Faulkner said, 'You never stop a running horse to give him sugar.'

"So he never did write me that or tell me that personally. April of '52 was the 90th anniversary of the Battle of Shiloh. I was on the way to the battleground and I was going through Oxford. I got there about 7:30 in the morning. I knew Faulkner was an early riser, so I went to the back door and knocked. He came out with about a week's growth of beard. He was wearing ragged clothes. I said, 'Mr. Faulkner, I'm going to drive up to Shiloh and I thought you might like to go along. ' He said, 'I would. It's a good idea. Excuse me a minute, I'll be right back.' He went upstairs and when he came back down, he was clean shaven, wearing his tweed jacket and that hat with the feather in it that he liked to wear. His handkerchief was tucked up his sleeve like an Englishman. And so we went on to Shiloh together.

"I took him where the 6th Mississippi made that charge with over 400 men and came out with just over 100. I told him that I had got myself a limb that weighed about nine pounds, the same as a rifle, and went charging up and down that hill to see what it was like.

"And he said that was just the way to do it.

"I have been to Shiloh a dozen times. The day I went with Faulkner I had been there four or five times. It is the most difficult of all battles to comprehend because, for one thing, it is in the woods. You get lost easily. And so did they—all 100,000 of them. Faulkner grasped it. I don't think he had ever been on that field before, but he grasped everything about it. Immediately.

Anybody else I have ever taken there can't begin to understand until they have had time to study it, but Faulkner latched right on to it. He had an unfailing sense of direction and immediate comprehension of the field and everything about it.

"He had been vaguely interested in the Civil War his whole life long. He was not a real student of it, but it fascinated him. His great-grandfather had been a colonel in the war at Shiloh, just like my great-grandfather. I'm always meeting people who say their great-great whatever was at Shiloh. Of course he was. They got ahold of every soldier they could find, from Pensacola, New Orleans, Memphis, everywhere else. My great-grandfather, Hezekiah William Foote, commanded the Noxubee cavalry at Shiloh.

"I spent that night at Faulkner's house. And I told him a ridiculous thing. He was amused by it, too. I said, 'You know, I have every right to expect to be a better writer than you are, because your models were Sherwood Anderson and Joseph Conrad. Mine are you and Marcel Proust. My writers are better than your writers.'

"He laughed. He did not point out the fact that it takes a third party too, you see."

Ironically, Shelby Foote has become something of a model himself. Since his appearance on the televised Civil War series, his voice, face, and narrative have become national treasures. "If southerners talk a lot about the Civil War," he says, "that's easy to account for. When I was coming along, if you had a difference of opinion with another boy, you had a fistfight. And I had many a one. The ones I remember with the greatest clarity are the ones I lost.

"And that is the way it is with the Civil War." Foote nods his head, smiles. "Yeah. That movie Patton, with George Patton standing out in front there with the big America flag behind him? He's got his lacquered helmet on, saying we Americans have never lost a war. Well, Patton's grandfather was in the Army of Northern Virginia, and he lost a war. And he's an American. The South has a tragic sense from having lost that war, not to mention the very practical sense of having lost all those men.

"I became interested in the Civil War very early. I used to read Civil War material at the same time I was reading the Rover Boys and Tom Swift and Tarzan. I guess it is only natural that it would interest me, though. Vicksburg was right down the road. And not only had I heard stories, but I used to see a few veterans in

Jefferson Davis's, Beauvoir, house down on the coast. It had been turned into an old soldier's home, the Confederate Veterans Home. I was a boy, 12 or 13 years old, and I'd go down there and talk to them, but I didn't know enough then. I remember one funny story. One of the veterans had lost a leg in the war. It was visitor's day and all the old ladies were coming by. Two old ladies stopped in front of the veteran and said, 'Oh, my good man, you've lost your leg.'

He looked down, too, and said, 'Damned if I haven't.'

"That's a Confederate soldier for you. That's the way they were. I also knew a lot of old ladies—old maids about 80 years old—who had lost their sweethearts in the Civil War.

"When Ken Burns did that television series, one of the reasons it was so good was that he had the narrative—the spoken, continuous narrative—already written. He sent it to about two dozen historians of the Civil War and asked them to read it. And he asked if they were willing to come to Washington to talk about it.

"So about 20 of us went up there and sat around this big table and went through that narrative page by page. Nothing could come up that six or seven historians there wouldn't know, whether it was Andersonville prison or whatever. Burns was immediately willing to drop anything for the sake of authenticity, no matter how much dramatic value it had. We all knew that he knew from the start that the closer he got to the truth, the better the thing was going to be."

After the program began to be televised, Foote was flooded with mail and telephone calls, so many that he gave up trying to respond. The financial rewards gave him the opportunity to continue writing without money problems. "I would worry about it if I didn't have it," he says, "but the only time you really need money is when you're dying." Foote taps his ever-present pipe and sighs. "I try not to be short-tempered about it. The only place where I draw the line is at signing books. And I certainly wouldn't go to one of those book signings at a book store. I think that is outrageous. Walker would sign anything in sight. He would go sit down in a book store and sign book after book after book. Yeah. He just didn't feel about it the way I do. For me, it seems like selling part of yourself for a little cash. Even the royalty. Fifteen percent of 25 dollars is money, and it sells books. I know a lot of writers who wished they hadn't done it. They go sit in the store there, and nobody comes. Yeah. Sell your soul, but can't find a buyer."

Foote not only had the good fortune to know Faulkner personally, he was lucky enough to understand the South as Faulkner understood it. Unfortunately, the Old South was rife with racial prejudice. "We ought to have felt guilt about it, but we didn't at the time. Most people bought the ridiculous theory that if it weren't for the white man, the Negro would have been running around in the jungle. They forgot that most of us came from peasant backgrounds in Europe." Foote points out that for the writer, though, slavery, no matter how unfair, created an advantage by creating an underclass. "Imagine a Russian novel without any peasants in it. I don't know where southern literature would have been without blacks to write about. It would be very different. A writer can place a value on terrible, terrible things. With the South and slavery, you had a society that was stacked up in different parts. That makes you conscious of your relationships with other people and what happens when their rules are crossed or broken. You have no grounds for moral indignation any more."

Foote says that in his youth, most southerners had the experience of bonding with blacks as childhood playmates. Beyond that, relationships usually did not continue. But a black woman who went to work for his Aunt Maude became Foote's loving friend. Her name was Nelly Lloyd. "Nelly meant as much to me as anybody on the face of this earth. She worked at Aunt Maude's house for 28 years, starting out at $2.50 a week. At the end of 28 years I think she was making either $12.50 or $15 a week. I was closer to her and spent more time with her than I did with anybody in my family. She raised me from early childhood to high school."

Greenville, though, was different from many other southern towns. "The Ku Klux Klan made no headway in Greenville. They got abolished about the time they got started. That was principally due to Senator Percy, who led the anti-Ku Klux forces in his campaign for the Senate. My mother's father was Jewish. The Jews in Greenville were among the leaders of the town in every sense. Anytime you would go to a corner store or the Elks Club or anywhere else, three out of ten people would be Jewish. There were more Jews in the Greenville Country Club than there were Baptists.

"While I was growing up, we didn't consider the question of race a problem because it didn't present itself as a problem. Everyone thought they were doing what they were supposed to do. Black people were servants, yard men, housekeepers, tenant farmers. We didn't consider they were mistreated, but they certainly were. Look at Nelly: worked all of 28 years and finally wound up making $15 a week. But, you also have to remember this was the Depression. A man making $250 a month could drive a Buick and belong to the country club. "

The problem of racial inequality didn't really hit Foote until he went to college at Chapel Hill. He was turned down for membership by Walker Percy's fraternity, SAE, because he had some Jewish blood in his veins. That didn't seem to bother him as much as the social position of the American Negro. " Walker and I were going to New York on a train and I told him that I thought something ought to be done about segregation and it should be done very soon, that blacks were citizens just as much as we were and all that foolishness ought to stop. Walker got furious. He said, 'And you call yourself a southerner?' This was 1937. Twenty years later, he was way out in front of me on this thing, but that was his reaction at the time."

Foote's maternal grandfather was Jewish, although his wife remained a Methodist. His paternal grandfather was also Methodist, but Foote was reared as an Episcopalian, as his father had been. Another prejudice prevalent in the early part of the century concerned marriages between Jews and non-Jews. "When that happened, the Jewish family would usually be more shocked because they wanted to preserve their identity," says Foote. "Mother's father had a fit when my mother and daddy eloped, although my daddy's father welcomed her. And eventually her own father got over it.

"My father's mother, whom I called Mammy, was very active in the Episcopal Church. She more or less took over that side of it, although my mother was anxious for me to strongly consider the Jewish religion. So I went to synagogue Sunday School for a few years and then made the shift myself. I figured life was hard enough without being Jewish too. I joined the Episcopal Church and was baptized and confirmed by Bishop Green, rest his soul. Now, though, I haven't had any religion in a very, very long time. No formal religion. I was an agnostic from the beginning. I never did buy into all that playing harps on clouds and all that stuff. I never went for that."

Whatever turn Foote's religious leanings have taken, the Bible has always been important to him. "I read the Bible along with Proust. I read it for its literary value. I was reading children's Bible stories as soon as I learned to read. They are wonderful stories. The story of Saul, for instance. You can't come close to that. But something even more important was the way they were told—the language: 'Remember now thy Creator in the days of thy youth, while the evil days come, and the years draw nigh, and thou shalt say I have no pleasure in them.' That knocks me off my feet."

Foote says that writing is like a religion to him. His life is governed by a belief in art. "That is where salvation is. Eternal life, anything you want to name. Freud says we write for three reasons: one of them is the love of women, another is money and the third is fame. Inspiration is not in there. I don't argue with that. I think most of the bad writing in the world, really bad writing, is done under the influence of what is called inspiration. It is terrible. Writing is a rigorous thing. It has to be learned by some very hard work. I was in a restaurant once with a doctor friend of mine. I said, 'You know, I think I have probably worked as hard learning my profession as you have learning yours. You could hear him laugh on the other side of town. He couldn't see that I had been doing any work at all. Walker used to say that people knew the Chevrolet dealer in Covington a lot better than they knew him. It's true, too. I think writers have a hard time nowadays. When I was coming along if you got a story printed in a magazine, you heard from three or four agents saying they had read your story and wanted to handle you in the future. Maybe the trouble nowadays is the simple fact that so many magazines have all disappeared, the *Saturday Evening Post, Colliers,* they are all gone."

Although Foote cannot recall a definitive moment when he decided to become a writer, he claims that he never considered anything else. "Except one time I thought I might be an architect. I never did know what a house was going to look like, but I liked arranging the rooms." Nor has he ever once considered leaving the South. "No. Not for an instant. I went to North Carolina to school and went wherever the Army sent me when I was in the service. But except for a brief period between the Army and the Marine Corps, I worked on the Associated Press local desk in New York and I rather enjoyed it. I had been there about four months before I realized I hadn't seen the sky and not the faintest suggestion of the moon in all this time. I was living up in Washington Heights. I'd come out the door, get on a subway, ride right on down to 50th Street, get out in the basement of the AP building, take the elevator up to the office. I just all of a sudden realized I wasn't in touch with the earth or the sky any more. Growing up in the South gave me something that is very real and I don't think we've lost it entirely. I think for the most part southerners are more polite, more gracious in their attitudes toward people and life itself. And I think that is a huge advantage. I've seen people in New York make their day by being rude to

somebody every now and then, and get enormous satis-
faction out of it. And the weather in the South gives you
more leisure time. Everybody knows that before air conditioning you didn't make any sudden movement or pick
up anything heavy. If you did you would fall out.

"I think the southern lifestyle involves an easier go
at things. There was less scrambling after money
because there was less money and there wasn't that
chance to make it. Our grandfathers and fathers had
been raised up under a terrible thing as a result of the
Civil War. From 1865 to 1934, freight rates were different in the North and South. That had a real serious economic impact on us. Many other things of that kind
went on as retaliation. It was a heavy load."

Shelby Foote's South is changing and his best friend
is gone, and gone with him is perhaps the biggest chunk
of Foote's life that anyone else has ever claimed, although the memories remain as vivid as ever. "Well,"
says Foote quietly, "Walker made a real good death. He
was at home. He wasn't in the hospital with tubes running in and out of him. His whole family was gathered
around him. I was there, too. He was in the last stages of
cancer, in terrible, terrible shape. But it was a good death.
I was glad to see him go, glad to see the suffering stop.
Walker made a full, good life. I don't miss him with any
pangs, I just miss him all the time. That's the way it is.

"I will never have another friend like that." He is
silent for a moment, then adds, "I haven't got another
60 years."

But nothing, not even Walker Percy's death, can
keep Shelby Foote from writing. "Yes. I'm always
writing something. Still write in longhand. I couldn't
write any other way." In the high-ceilinged room

where he works, bookshelves cover the entire wall on one side. The opposite wall is lined with windows that look out onto the garden below. A third wall is dominated by a magnificent old fireplace over which hangs a huge modern abstract painting. A bed is pushed up against the fourth wall, and next to it hangs the revered portrait of Proust.

Shelby Foote has never owned a computer. He says, "I have enough trouble with that electric type-writer. A computer would drive me around the corner." From the shelf above his desk, he pulls out a bound copy book. Inside is page after page of beauti-fully hand-scribed text so perfect it looks almost like calligraphy. "That's a fair copy that I make at the end of each day. Then I have them bound up when I get through and I type from that copy.

"I am a southern writer," Foote says proudly. He points to the portrait of Proust. "That is a Parisian writer. So, it doesn't bother me a-tall to be called southern.

"I don't consider that I should have any judgment on present day southern writing because it couldn't be as bad as I think it is. There are plenty of exceptions. Rich-ard Ford is a good writer. There are good writers around, but with the exception of Cormac McCarthy, I can't find anybody of the stature I was accustomed to when Faulkner and the rest of them were going full speed ahead.

I would bet, though, that when Theodore Dreiser died, a great many Americans said, 'Literature is dead,' and there were Faulkner and Hemingway and Fitzgerald going full blast, writing away like mad, better than Dreiser ever dreamed of being. So, I don't trust myself on that. I'm crazy about Eudora Welty's work, but Carson McCullers is my favorite of the women writers.

"They say Southerners are always talking about the Civil War. It is true, but not as true as they say. I've been at a table with New Yorkers at nightclubs or restaurants, and one of them will say, "You southerners are always talking about the Civil War. Now, I haven't mentioned the Civil War, mind you. He has mentioned the Civil War.

"One night I had some fun with them. This was back in the early '50s. About six or seven of us were sitting around the table talking, and somebody had to say, "You are from Mississippi, aren't you?"

I said, "Yes."

"What in the world do you do down there?"

I said, "Not much."

"So, how can you stand it?"

"Well, we've got certain things down there that amount to something. For example, who do you think is the best writer in the United States?"

"William Faulkner."

"He's from Mississippi. Who do you think is the best woman writer in the United States?"

"Eudora Welty."

"Well, she's from Mississippi. Who do you think the greatest playwright in America?"

"Tennessee Williams."

"He's from Mississippi."

So I said, "I guess we do do a few things down there."

Now, those who repeat Foote's anecdote have another Mississippian to add to the list. When someone asks, 'Who do you think is the greatest chronicler of the Civil War?' the answer will be immediate and unqualified: Shelby Foote

Excerpt from *Shiloh*:

The sky had cleared, the clouds raveled to tatters, and at four o'clock the sun broke through, silver on the bright green of grass and leaves and golden on the puddles in the road; all down the column men quickened the step, smiling in the sudden burst of gold and silver weather. They would point at the sky, the shining fields, and call to each other: the sun, the sun! Their uniforms, which had darkened in the rain, began to steam in the April heat, and where formerly they had slogged through the mud, keeping their eyes down on the boots or haversack of the man ahead, now they began to look around and even dance aside with little prancing steps to avoid the wet places. As we rode past at the side of the road, they cheered and called out to us: "You better keep up there! Don't get left behind!" Replacing their hats from cheering the general, they jeered at me especially, since I was the youngest and brought up the rear. "Jog on, sonny. If you lose him you'll never find him again!"

This was mainly a brown country, cluttered with dead leaves from the year before, but the oaks had tasseled and the redbud limbs were like flames in the wind. Fruit trees in cabin yards, peach and pear and occasional quince, were sheathed with bloom, white and pink, twinkling against broken fields and random cuts of new grass washed clean by the rain. Winding over and among the red clay hills, the column had strung out front and rear, accordion action causing it to clot in places and move spasmodically in others, as if the road itself had come alive, had been sowed with the dragon teeth of olden time, and was crawling like an enormous snake toward Pittsburg Landing.

Seen that way, topping a rise and looking back and forward, it was impersonal: an army in motion, so many inspissated tons of flesh and bone and blood and equipment: but seen from close, the mass reduced to company size in a short dip between two hills, it was not that way at all. I could see their faces then, and the army became what it really was: forty thousand men—they were young men mostly, lots of them even younger than myself, and I was nineteen just two weeks before—out on their first march in the crazy weather of early April, going from Mississippi into Tennessee where the Union army was camped between two creeks with its back to a river, inviting destruction.

Phot by Fred Brown.

Photography courtesy of Lee Smith.

LEE SMITH

"The mountains which used to imprison me have become my chosen stalking ground."

As soon as she opens her mouth to speak, you are pulled in, poised to listen. She fixes her bright blue eyes on your face and you sense immediately that she is your best friend, you can tell her anything, and you do. Her voice, slightly flat and slowed by a distinct drawl, wraps around you, rising in excitement so that many of her statements seem like questions. While she talks, her hands fly back and forth, fluttering and gesturing, sometimes measuring, sometimes opening expansively, sometimes pushing back her long hair, which is blonde and streaked with gray. And before you even realize that she is telling you a story, she has pulled you into it the way she pulls you into her stories on paper, the ones she has typed on her old electric Smith Corona with the broken *s*. It is Lee Smith at her best.

"The way southerners tell a story is really specific to the South," Smith says. "It's a whole narrative strategy, it's an approach. Every kind of information is imparted in the form of a story." Ask for directions in the South? She laughs. "It's not just *Turn left.* It's *I remember the time my cousin went up there and got bit by a mad dog.*

29

It's a whole different approach to interactions between people and to transmitting information."

Nobody in Grundy, Virginia, ever doubted that Lee Smith would grow up to be a famous storyteller, especially not Smith herself, who says she has been " romantically dedicated" to the grand idea of being a writer ever since she could remember.

Smith was what you'd call a "late" baby—in fact she was a surprise baby—born to Ernest Lee Smith and his wife Virginia (Gig, pronounced Jig) in the southwest coal-mining town of Grundy Virginia on November 1, 1944. Ernest Lee, then 38, was in the Navy in New Guinea on the day his only child was born, and Gig, 37, a home economics teacher, had gone to the hospital a few days early to wait for the birth. To calm her restlessness, she had spent the time baking biscuits for the other patients. "My parents were so delighted to have a child," Smith claims, "they thought anything I did was wonderful. If I had announced I wanted to be an axe murderer, they would have said, 'Great!' But fortunately, it was, "You want to be a writer? Great!"

Smith says that the narrator, Karen, in her story, "Tongues of Fire," is as close to an autobiographical double as any character she has created. Like Karen, Smith often pictured herself ". . . poised at the foggy edge of a cliff someplace in the south of France, wearing a cape, drawing furiously on a long cigarette, hollow-cheeked and haunted."

In the 27 years of Smith's adult writing life, she has become perhaps the foremost voice in Appalachian fiction today. Most of her characters are based on people she grew up with, or on characters she heard about in her childhood.

"I came from a very talkative family," Smith says. "Nobody read, but everybody talked a whole lot. My father told most of the stories, but my Uncle Vern was a real storyteller, too. And so were different neighbors, especially a man down the street named Harold Trivett and my best friend's father, Habern Owens. My dad told me mountain stories in particular. My Aunt Ruth would tell me stories, and my mother, who had lived in Grundy for 50 years by the time she died, was always telling me something about somebody in town. Every time I went home after I had gone away to school, or after I was grown, I'd write those stories down."

Smith says that for a southerner, physical surroundings encompass much more than a town or a region. She cites place and voice as the most important elements in storytelling. "Everybody has a very strong sense of place," she says, "but in the South that implies who you are and what your family did. It's not just literally the physical surroundings, what stuff looks like. It's a whole sense of the past.

"Place is so important to me. I can never imagine a book without a place. Even if I write a short story, I have to make diagrams of what the character's house looks like and where the house is in relation to the town. Putnam's just sent me a map I used when I wrote *Oral History.*" She picks up her dark-rimmed reading glasses, rummages through some papers on her desk, finds the big hand-drawn map of Hoot Owl Holler and its environs. With that map you could find your way to any of the characters—Almarine, Dory, Ora Mae, Pricey Jane, Red Emmy. You could climb Black Rock Mountain, find your way to Grassy Creek or the Smith Hotel where Richard Burlage stayed. For each section of the book there is a family tree, so that the reader can keep track of the characters that Lee Smith knows intimately even before she sits down to write the first word.

In order to keep her writing spontaneous, she rarely revises. Even when her characters are flawed human beings, she gives the reader a little something to love in each one.

Despite the changing face of the South from rural agrarian to urban industrialized, Smith says that the style of her writing students at the University of North Carolina is still essentially regional. "The way they are southern is different, but they are still very southern. For example, I might have a student who has grown up at the mall in Fayetteville and her parents have split up and she's lived a lot of places, but she writes a story which, though it doesn't take place in a small town, still has a voice that is thoroughly southern. Southerners have a way of approaching facts and information and shaping them into a form that is a natural story. As small towns disappear and rural life changes as the South changes, a twenty-year-old will have a sense of place that is different from the sense of place that we who grew up in the South had years earlier. But that particular voice will still be there. It will be different from ours, because so few people were lucky enough to grow up in the kind of closed and special circumstances we had, but it will still be southern."

In the isolated little mountain town of Grundy where she was born, Smith grew up steeped in stories, inundated, but her early imagination carried her beyond the hills of Grundy—to settings in exotic places like Hawaii. She wrote about stewardesses, imaginary universes, evil twins. When she left home for St. Catherine's Girls'

School, and later, for Hollins College in Richmond, she never once considered using Grundy as a setting or shaping a character after any of the unique citizens of the town. Finally it was her voracious appetite for reading that steered her toward her natural style. As a child she had begun an ambitious reading plan, starting with the A's in the library and reading steadily through the alphabet, so she wouldn't miss anything important. By the time she had worked her way to the S's as a student at Hollins, she made a discovery that changed her very future: In the stacks under the S's she found the work of James Still, whose novel *River of Earth* follows the Baldridge family's heartbreaking struggle to survive when their crops fail and the mines close. Smith had begun to see such occurrences reflected in her own home town as Grundy suffered a slow economic deterioration. When she came to the end of Still's novel, she was amazed to discover that the Baldridges were heading to Grundy to work in the mines.

Grundy! In a book! In print and published! Smith later recorded her reactions in a feature article in the *Charlotte News & Observer:* "Suddenly, lots of the things of my life occurred to me for the first time as stories: my mother and my aunts sitting on the porch talking endlessly about whether one of them had colitis or not; Hardware Breeding, who married his wife, Beulah, four times; how my uncle Curt taught my daddy to drink good liquor; how I got saved at the tent revival; John Hardin's hanging in the courthouse square; how Pete Chaney rode the flood . . . .

"I started to write these stories down. Twenty-five years later, I'm still at it. And it's a funny thing: Though I have spent most of my life in universities, though I live in Chapel Hill and eat pasta and drive a Toyota, the stories which present themselves to me as worth the telling are most often those somehow connected to that place and those people. The mountains which used to imprison me have become my chosen stalking ground."

That was the epiphany. Smith had at last found her real and most evocative voice—her Appalachian voice. She began to interview her family about Grundy's history and gossip and ghosts. On every visit back home she gleaned more information—truth, supposition, hearsay, and facts that sooner or later would find their way into her stories. For a long time—since childhood, in fact—she had been an observer of character, had mastered voice and had literally lived in her own scenes, but James Still's work had opened up a floodgate of new possibilities.

Because Smith's stories now come from her very background, her involvement with her characters is sometimes a personal odyssey, often a journey of love. During the writing of *Fair and Tender Ladies,* a book inspired by a packet of real letters she discovered at a garage sale, she became so close to the character of Ivy Rowe that she was loathe to finish the book. It was only on the repeated insistence of her publishers that she finally agreed to give it over to them. The voice of Ivy Rowe personifies more than any other of Smith's characters the woman whose ascendance from childhood to womanhood represents a typical Appalachian woman's journey through life. Smith says that that character, more than anything else, helped her deal with the death of her mother.

From the beginning of her career, Smith's narrative voice has reflected her keen ear for accent and inflection.

In a review of *Oral History,* Smith's highly acclaimed novel of 1983, Christopher Lehmann-Haupt said that "what Lee Smith does best of all in this multi-generational family history is to capture the voices that tell her story. . . . Her mimicry is perfect. The rural folk it treats may long ago have been turned into cliches by imitators of William Faulkner, Flannery O'Connor and Eudora Welty, but in *Oral History* Lee Smith brings them back to life again."

Smith had discovered that to achieve that resurrection, she had only to remember the voices from her childhood and then let the characters speak in their own voices.

Her appreciation for detail showed up early in her career. At the age of 11, Smith and her best friend Martha Sue Owens "published" a neighborhood newspaper, *The Small Review,* which they laboriously hand-copied for 12 neighbors. In the paper the girls wrote up "newsworthy events" that occurred in Cowtown, the section of Grundy where they lived. In a 1954 issue, the author noted: "Lee Smith and Martha Sue Owens went shopping at Kings Department Store in Bristol, Tennessee, to buy their school clothes. Lee Smith got to look at her feet through a machine to see if her shoes fit." The Review also featured a regular column, "This is Your Life," in which one of the townspeople was always featured. In "This is Your Life, William Germaine Burkes," Smith reported, "You met Stella Artrep at Skeet Rock. You were married and lived in Clintwood, while you practiced dentistry in adjoining coal fields."

Sometimes her observations got her into trouble. The controversial editorial, "George McGuire Is Too Grumpy," exacted an apology to the neighbor across the street, but Smith has never worried much about censure from her large extended family. "They didn't read books when I was growing up," she says. "They still don't, so I can write anything without hurting their feelings, because they'll never see it."

The same careful attention to detail that appeared in her childhood newspaper turns up in all her novels and stories. In *Fancy Strut* she writes:

> Bob and Frances Pitt stayed in a bridal suite in the Ocean-Aire Autel at Fort Walton Beach, Florida, on their honeymoon, and had a perfectly all right time; but do you know what Johnny B. and Sandy DuBois did? They went to the Southern 500 at Darlington, South Carolina, and sat out in the weather on those old hard benches for three entire days, watching the cars go around and around.

Religion and religiosity played an enormous role in shaping Lee Smith's work. In the rural South, tent revivals are loud and lively social events, converts are "saved" in dramatic and emotional surrender to Jesus, fundamentalists speak in tongues and sometimes handle serpents, and children are taught that the devil is as real as the next door neighbor. In *Oral History,* the schoolteacher Richard Burlage describes a church service in Tug:

> For here is a phenomenon: this most expressionless of people, who pride themselves . . . in showing neither hunger, nor pain, nor grief—these people certainly 'let go' in church. At length the women begin rocking back and forth, there is a kind of collective sobbing, and often someone will rush forward at the invitation to be 'saved from the fiery pit of hell and them little old licking flames,' as Autry Lily pictures it in his characteristic language.

Smith says that her spiritual life was not so much devotional as emotional. "I loved Sunday school, but I associated church with my grandparents, since we sat with them every Sunday, third pew from the back on the left-hand side of the little stone Methodist church which my grandfather had attended all his life, which my grandmother had attended since their marriage fifty years before. Usually my mother went to church too . . . usually my father attended only on Easter. Frankly, I liked those Sundays when none of them made it, when Mama just dropped me off in front of the church and I went in all alone, clutching my quarter for the collection plate, to sit with my grandparents. Even though I was invisible in my own family, my grandparents noticed me plenty. I was their good, good little girl . . . certainly, I felt, their favorite. I did everything I could to ensure that this was true."

In her eleventh year, Smith found her greatest excitement in being saved. Again and again she gave herself publicly to Christ, until the constant dedication became an embarrassment to her parents. She had a friend at school who lived in a "holler" and whose mother spoke in tongues. "I loved it," says Smith. "I told my mother I wanted to start speaking in tongues. When she heard that, she sent me to summer camp to get me away from my friend's influence."

At camp Smith immediately contracted bronchitis. Sick, depressed, and homesick, she had what was described as a "fit" at the Episcopalian vespers service and later announced that she had heard the voice of God. The camp administrators, declaring the child "disturbed," put her in the infirmary and called her parents. Gig promised Lee that if she swore not to talk about hearing God anymore, she would buy her a Pekingese dog.

But that was not the end of her religiosity. When Smith was in high school, she accompanied friends to churches of various denominations and was "saved" at nearly every house of worship in town. Her mother defused the situation by threatening not to let her use the family car unless she stopped courting chronic salvation.

In *Black Mountain Breakdown,* Smith describes Crystal's salvation:

> Crystal rises . . . . She's sure she'll throw up, but then she doesn't and she's moving steadily, blindly down the dirt aisle, tripping over wires, straight to Fred Lee Sampson where he stands holding out his arms. 'O Lamb of God, I come, I come,' they sing. Crystal reaches Fred Lee Sampson and falls on her knees at his feet. Every part of her mind and body is on fire, flaming, a keen high white flame like a giant Bunsen burner in the chemistry lab, all through her. Crystal is nothing but flame.

"Religion," says Smith," has always been a very emotional thing for me. I felt that I had to either give myself over to it completely or leave it alone. I've always been both attracted and repelled by the idea of turning yourself over to a greater thing. It's a real danger for women, anyway. When I got to St. Catherine's, everything was Episcopalian, and actually, I liked it because I was getting kind of worn out, and I backed off, and it was a relief not to be so emotional. Then in college I was exposed to all kinds of ideas and nobody I knew was very religious—they were all kind of arty— and I didn't go to church much anymore, although now I do go some, and I'm always writing about it."

In some way, nearly all of Smith's characters think a great deal about religion. For example, in *Saving Grace,* Grace declares, "Daddy and Mama talked about Jesus all the time. I loved Daddy and Mama, but I did not love Jesus—I was scared of Jesus."

When she talks about religion, Smith's expressive face turns serious. "That's one of the things I'm always worrying about. I mean, what is the purpose and what are we supposed to do? How do you live a good life and does God really exist? I can't leave it alone. I'm always worrying about it and thinking about it and I have to say I don't have the kind of faith that I had as a child. It does seem to me very arbitrary, and terrible things happen to really good people, and you can't understand it. I guess the only thing you can do is do the best you can and be as good a person as you possibly can, if you can even figure out what that means. In *Saving Grace* I've written about somebody who gives himself over to God completely, and I think I wrote that book because I can't do it. A lot of times people write out things that they wish they could do themselves. I would like to think there is a great master plan, but I don't actually. It seems pretty chaotic to me. Some of my characters think there is a master plan, and there's a part of me that thinks it, but then again things will happen that make you wonder, If there is a master plan, how in the hell does this part fit in?"

A prayer book presented to Smith by Opie C. Clarke, pastor of Grundy Methodist Church in 1962, when Smith was 17, has a blue felt Methodist Youth Fellowship banner as a bookmark. The place marked is page 27, and it is a prayer entitled "For Holy Speech." It reads: "Let me speak with sincerity, Lord. Help me to be honest with myself, as well as with others." Whether

Smith read the prayer or not, she recounts this story: "My father was fond of saying that I would climb a tree to tell a lie rather than stand on the ground to tell the truth. In fact, in the mountains where I come from, a lie was often called a story, and well do I remember being shaken until my teeth rattled and given the stern admonition: "Don't you tell me no story, now!"

Smith couldn't help it. She was born a storyteller and as soon as she was able to spell, she started writing. "Writing stories gave me a special power, I felt." Her first "novel," written on her mother's stationery when Smith was eight years old, had as its main characters her two favorite people—Adlai Stevenson and Jane Russell. The plot involved their falling in love and heading west in a covered wagon. When they reached their destination, they converted to Mormonism.

"I had a really privileged happy childhood and teen-aged years," Smith recounts. Active in various club organizations and county representative for the 4-H Club (she was selected because of her expertise in making potato salad), she was a cheerleader and was elected Miss Grundy High. In 1963, when she was nineteen, she was second-place winner in the annual Miss Buchanan County Beauty Pageant. "It was kind of an ideal life," she says, looking back. "My whole family was all around, I had a boyfriend I was crazy about, I never had a sense of being deprived or uninteresting."

It was not until she had actually left home that Lee Smith realized how isolated—and insulated—she had been in Grundy. Relatives lived on both sides of her house and across the street. She had about 50 cousins to associate with, and aunts and uncles all chipped in to help when things went awry. "My cousins all went into the grocery business," says Smith. "In Grundy if you didn't have a store, you were in mining. There were strip mines and deep mines and coke ovens, but obviously everything revolved around coal mining. I was a town girl but I always had real good friends who lived up in the hollers and whose daddies were actually working in the mines. My cousins lived in a company town, but their daddy was an engineer, so they had a flush toilet." But, Smith says, for the most part Grundy was so poor that it lacked the kind of hierarchical social aristocracy entrenched in many other southern towns. "When I went to college and read Faulkner," she says, "it was like reading about Guatemala." In Grundy there were no black people, and there was absolutely no sense of class.

Geographically, Grundy is physically isolated. It was even more remote before Route 460 was built. Even today, Grundy sometimes seems to outsiders like the end of the world. In his book *Salvation on Sand Mountain,* Dennis Covington describes his trip through Grundy on a journey to a snake-handling church service in Jolo, West Virginia:

> Once the road narrowed and entered the mountains, the signs disappeared, replaced by mine tipples, mantrips, and long lines of train cars filled with coal that steamed in the rain. The last motels and hospital were at Grundy, Virginia, a mining town on the lip of a winding river between mountains so steep and irrational, they must have blocked most of the sun most of the day. It is difficult to imagine how children can grow up in such a place without carrying narrowed horizons into the rest of their lives.

Lee Smith never felt deprived, but there was a difficult factor in her childhood that she never talked about while her parents were still alive. Both her parents suffered from serious mental depression and were frequently hospitalized. But Smith says in Grundy, there was no stigma attached to their illnesses. "It was just a part of my life."

Yet it was not without its dark moments. Whenever her father started on one of his cycles, he would simply say he felt "kindly nervous."

"My dad would probably be diagnosed today as manic depressive," Smith says, "but with him the manic phase was not fun, he was just a workaholic. Those periods would be followed by periods when he was just prostrate, when he was depressed and couldn't speak. Usually it was a big cycle. The big, hard stuff—the real breakdowns—started when I was 10 or 11.

"My mother, too, suffered from anxiety and depression, so she was also in and out of the hospital. Her father had killed himself, and one of her brothers had killed himself. There was all this going on, but it didn't really seem to affect me. They didn't make me a part of the whole constellation. There were several periods where my father or mother would be in the hospital for months at a time, and everybody in the family would pitch in and take care of things for them, run the dime store, come over to the house and take care of me. In his older years Daddy grew out of it, though he took Elavil to the end of his life.

"Mama and Daddy were always totally supportive of each other. They had the perfect system, and I wasn't included. It went on all during my childhood. One year they were both in the hospital at the same time for the whole year and I went to live with an aunt up in Maryland. Daddy was in the Duke psychiatric ward, Mama was at the University of Virginia, sometimes Shepherd Pratt, and Daddy was at Silver Hill in Connecticut. That never once struck me as even unusual. For example, the next door neighbor was always having shock treatments. I have been told that the people I write about are eccentric, but I never really thought they were. It was what I grew up with, and it has had some influence on my characters, but it was all sort of out in the open. Nobody ever tried to keep it a secret."

To deal with the disruptions, "I wrote all the time, made up huge complicated things. With my cousin, I had this big detective game that involved everybody in town. We were always going around leaving clues on everybody's windshield wipers. There was a huge megaplot that I was in charge of. And then we had a theater. We'd put up a shower curtain on somebody's breezeway and we would write plays and act them out and make everybody pay to come and see them.

"I had tons of imaginary friends. Sylvia was my best imaginary friend. My mother had to set a place for her at the table, and we had these big discussions when we were going to go somewhere as to whether Sylvia was going to come along. I think I was really a very phobic child. Some of that is reflected in *Black Mountain Breakdown.* I had a different ghost for every night of the week. The first book I wrote, *The Last Day the Dogbushes Bloomed,* was very much about the kind of child I was, my fears and thoughts. Ritualistic behavior wards off terrors, and I did a lot of that.

"I write for self-repair. A lot of times I don't really know why I'm writing what I'm writing until several years later, and I will find out that in fact I was working through something in my life." For example, Smith's first book *(Dogbushes)* was about a little girl who is very very imaginative and then she gives up the world of the imagination in order to live in the real world. "It is sort of painful to do that," says Smith, "and I wrote that book when I was in college. It was a way to deal with those issues, because you know, when you are real imaginative, you are almost crazy, and there's a fine line there. That was my way of distancing myself from the child and becoming more firmly an adult. When both your parents are crazy, you are always afraid that you are going to go crazy, too. Writing has been very helpful for me because it has been a way to channel all that crazy stuff."

Smith's official birth date is listed as November 1, 1944. She says she was actually born the day before, but her mother insisted on the November 1 date so that her daughter would not have to live under the stigma of having been born on Halloween.

A photograph of the house she grew up in shows a pleasant pale yellow two-story dormer with two chimneys, two porches, and green shutters. The house was one in a row of homes situated along the Levisa River, but children of the town were forbidden to play in the river, because upstream, the coal companies washed coal in it, dying the water black.

The mountains that rise so majestically behind the house in the photograph were so steep, Smith recalls, "that the sun never shone on my mother's roses before eleven o'clock in the morning. Mama hated this. She came from the flat exotic Eastern Shore of Virginia, and she swore that the mountains gave her migraine headaches and colitis. Mama was always lying down on the sofa, all dressed up. But there was no question that she loved my father, a mountain man who came from right there in Buchanan County, from a big family of whiskey-drinking, story-telling Democrats who used to sit out on my grandmother's porch every Sunday after dinner placing fifty-dollar bets on which bird would fly first off the telephone wire."

In "Fire and Ice," an unpublished piece that Smith wrote for a PEN fund-raiser, Smith wrote:

> My mother suffered from ideas of aristocracy. . . . Every night she would fix a nice supper for Daddy and me, then bathe and put on a fresh dress and high heels and her bright red lipstick, named Fire and Ice, and then sit in anxious dismay while the hour grew later and later, until Daddy finally left his dimestore and came home.
>
> By that time the food had dried out to something crunchy and unrecognizable in the oven, so Mama would cry when she opened the oven door, but then Daddy would eat it all anyway, swearing it was the most delicious food he'd ever put in his mouth, staring hard at Mama all the while, and paying absolutely no attention to me, who had stayed up so late to tell him something very important. Frequently my parents would then leave the table abruptly, feigning huge yawns and leaving me to turn out all the lights. I'd stomp around the house . . . both horrified and thrilled at the thought of them upstairs behind their closed door, actually kissing each other right on the mouth where you eat.

Gig Smith had definite ideas about propriety. A lady never lets a silence fall, she told her daughter. Horses sweat, men perspire, and women glow. She would often send Lee down to Birmingham to learn how to be a lady from her Aunt Gay Gay. Smith laughs at the memory.

"Aunt Gay Gay used to say, 'Let's have a drink. It's already dark underneath the house.'"

Smith's grandmother Chloe (pronounced Clo) Smith, never appeared in public without dressing up. In the story "Artists," Smith patterned the grandmother after Chloe:

> . . . She wore hats and white gloves on every possible occasion. Her manner of dress had changed so little over the years that even I could recognize its eccentricity. She dressed up all the time. I never saw her in my life without her pale voile or silk or brocade dresses, without her stockings, without her feet crammed into elegant shoes at least two sizes too small for her, so that at the end her feet were actually crippled. I never saw her without her makeup or the flashing rhinestone earrings and brooches and bracelets that finally she came to believe—as I believed then—were real.

All of the Smith family had to visit Grandmother Smith every single day. "It was required," Smith recalls.

Early on, Smith was criticized for making her female characters stronger than the males, but the spunk those characters exhibit in their girlhoods always becomes tempered by the strains of motherhood in rural Appalachia. Smith saw examples of this spiritual erosion every day in Grundy. "Women were closed in by the mountains and by their families. It was difficult for them, being bound biologically and geographically, to free themselves from the constrictions of male society. In *Black Mountain Breakdown* Crystal Spangler is unable to free herself from the things that bind her and she ends up being paralyzed. *The Devil's Dream* is about a woman who is freed geographically, is able to sing her own songs, produce her own records, but at a cost. One of those costs is that she loses touch with her family.

"My mother," says Smith, "was involved in a lot of activities—she belonged to just about every organization in Grundy—but I don't think you could say she was independent because she was very much bound by her sense of how she ought to behave. Most of the women I knew were like that except for a few of the wilder ones, some of the mountain women, but not the ones in town who were my mother's good friends. I remember that in Grundy there were girls who got pregnant and had to get married and by the time they were 25 years old they had a bunch of children and they looked awful and seemed "down" when you talked to them and there wasn't much they were ever going to be able to do about it.

"I had a lot of close relationships with women friends and girlfriends. When you are an only child, you sort of idealize the sibling relationship. I always have all these sisters in my books because I never had any in real life. Silvaney in *Fair and Tender Ladies* has been called an alter ego. And in a way she really is the other side of Ivy."

Despite the strong matriarchal figures in Smith's life, she was extremely close to her father, who died in 1992. "My daddy was real handsome," Smith says, smiling. "He was sort of "the king of Grundy" because he owned the Ben Franklin dime store, but more so because he was just so sweet. He knew everybody, and I was known because of him.

"He read out loud to me a whole lot. He would get drunk and read Kipling—"The Face on the Barroom Floor" and "The Road to Mandalay"—that kind of thing."

Some of Smith's fondest memories revolve around time spent at the Ben Franklin store. In a piece called "Illusions," she wrote:

> My favorite memory from childhood takes place at the dimestore. It is a Sunday afternoon near Easter, and the store is officially closed but the basement is full of women working overtime to assemble Easter baskets. I help for a while, and then I get sleepy. The women don't pay me much mind. They're busy talking, and before long they have gotten off onto one of my all-time favorite topics: having babies. I hear all about a terrible britches-baby, which is how they refer to a breech birth, and about a baby girl born with a veil, and doomed to know the future in her breast. I sink down and down into a big box of pink cellophane straw which drifts and settles until it covers me entirely and when I look up, all I can see is a pink dazzle of fluorescent light. All I can hear is those women's voices, telling stories. That Sunday afternoon seemed to go on forever and ever.

As a child Smith read not for entertainment or information, she says, but "to feel all wild and trembly inside." Her favorites were "anything at all about horses and saints." Other books that affected Smith were *Little Women,* especially the part where Beth dies, and *Gone with the Wind,* especially the part where Melanie dies. She also loved *Marjorie Morningstar, A Tree Grows in Brooklyn, Heidi,* and books like *Dear and Glorious Physician, The Shoes of the Fisherman,* and *Christy.* "All the kids' stuff—all the Nancy Drew books. The Bible. Nobody ever told me something was too old for me because they didn't know, see, they hadn't read them. I would read stuff that would have made my mother die—*Mandingo,* Frank Yerby; *Raintree County* put me to bed for about two days. I had to lie down.

"When Marguerite Henry was writing *Misty of Chincoteague* and Leslie Dennis was illustrating it, they stayed at my grandmother's boarding house on Chincoteague Island and the people who owned the horse Misty were distant cousins—the Barbies—and we would go to see Misty."

Smith associates poetry with her grandmother, who, being "cultured," owned a book of onehundred and one famous poems. "But once I got into it myself," Smith says, "Yeats was the one I always loved. Now I read poetry all the time."

As a teenager Smith had a boyfriend, but she was also in love with Habern Owens, her best friend's father, who lived three houses down the road. "Habern Owens had huge dark soulful eyes and thick black hair and a moustache that drooped down on either side of his mouth, and the prettiest singing voice available. Every night after supper, he'd sit out in his garden by the river and play his guitar and sing the old songs for Martha and me and every other kid in the neighborhood. "He was the only man in the neighborhood who didn't work, and Smith understood her mother to say that it was because he had romantic fever. "But of course she had said *rheumatic* fever. He died when Martha and I were fourteen, and neither one of us ever got over it."

After an early marriage to poet James Seay that ended in divorce, Smith has found happiness with journalist Hal Crowther. Their close-knit family includes Smith's two sons, Josh and Page, and Crowther's daughter.

In 1992 Smith's father closed the dimestore after 46 years in business, and on the last day of his going-out-of-business sale, he went home, had a stroke, and died five days later. Smith writes about her father's death in "Illusions":

> This did not happen to Adlai Stevenson or Jane Russell or any character I ever made up. It happened to my father, Ernest Smith, age 84, on September 5, 1992.
>
> I cannot write any story that will change it. I cannot keep the dimestore open, or keep my father alive. But I know I will go on writing stories, for they are as necessary to me now as breathing. This is the only way I can live my life. And though I know it is an illusion—for nothing can stay time—I will fix on a piece of paper someplace, in some story, that Sunday dimestore, and those women telling about the baby born with the veil, and myself looking up through the pink Easter straw into a future that held only light.

Excerpt from *Oral History:*

> In spite of him being so pretty, with all that pale-gold hair, in spite of him being no trouble to a living soul, Almarine was said to spend nights in the laurel slick over by Frenchman's Cave, nights by hisself out there when he was not but nine or ten. Now that's the wild side of Black Rock Mountain. And Almarine knowed where Grassy Creek starts, away up there where it comes a-bubbling and a-snorting like a regular fountain right out of the ferny ground. Almarine went beyond that spring, too, straight up the rocky clift where the trees won't grow and this little fine green grass grows all around in a perfect circle. A lot of folks won't go up there. But Almarine went and lived to tell it and went again, and nobody marked his com-

ings or goings in particular, or cared how he could scream in the night like a painter until the painters all around were screaming back. Almarine trained a crow one time, till it could talk. It could say about fifteen words when his brother Riley kilt it with a rifle, out of spite. That's how Riley was. But Almarine! Almarine had the lightest, biggest eyes when he was a little child. It seemed like he never blinked. He liked to look out on some distance.

Almarine didn't need nobody, is what it was, and there's folks won't take to a child like that. Still and all, he was sweet when nobody else in that family was, so this was a part of it too. People don't like somebody to be so sweet it makes them look bad, that's a fact. Which he was. I mean he was that sweet. In fact Almarine was that kind of sweet moony child who'll like end up without a thing in this or any other world, without a pot to piss in.

BOOKS BY LEE SMITH:

The Last Day the Dogbushes Bloomed
Something in the Wind
Fancy Strut
Black Mountain Breakdown
Oral History
Family Linen
Fair and Tender Ladies
The Devil's Dream
Saving Grace
Cakewalk
Me and My Baby View the Eclipse
The Christmas Letters

Photo by Fred Brown.

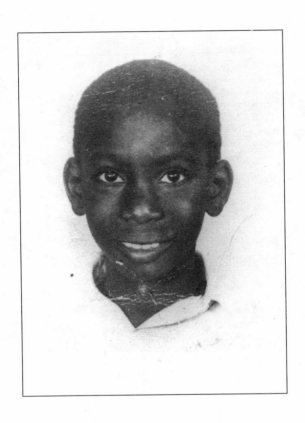

YUSEF KOMUNYAKAA

"There was an immense silence about race. Blacks didn't even talk about it among themselves. My father didn't talk about it. In my generation they questioned it, but there was no answer."

Yusef Komunyakaa is a man full of rhythms. He is tall and elegant, with skin so dark that when his face breaks into a crooked smile, it is like a light coming on. His long stride, his gestures and movements, seem as graceful and measured as the meter in his prize-winning poetry, and when he reads aloud, his voice rolls out in an voluminous baritone song.

That voice, like his poetry, seems to emerge from an ancient ground where it has been growing for generations, fertile and essential. And sometimes through the poet's throat rises the resonant voice of his people, living and dead.

Komunyakaa is a man who has often lived on the edge of danger, but through some deep inner reserve, he has since childhood been able to coax himself away from chaos to order and serenity. The danger is still there, though, reflected in the fervent message of his work and in the passionate electricity of its syntax. Somehow it teaches us that just beneath the surface of beauty lies violence, and that violence often has a peculiar beauty of its own.

Komunyakaa is no stranger to violence, having experienced it at home in Bogalusa, Louisiana, where it was a daily presence during his childhood, and in Vietnam, where the difference was that the enemy was a stranger. "In America when we mention cities," he says, "people say, 'Oh, violence!' But think about rural violence. There is much more violence in rural areas than in cities. We as Americans haven't really dealt with that. I'm talking about how graphic and precise it is, how it is thought out and planned. I'm not just talking about slitting the throat of a hog, an event I participated in when I was six or seven, I'm talking about overall violence within the family."

How did he survive the violence of his father, J.W., whose wife—Yusef's mother—finally escaped the wild domination of her husband and left behind her six bewildered children? How did he survive the brutish inhumanity of Vietnam, where his best friend was killed by enemy bullets? How did he survive being a poor black man in a white man's South and emerge as a Pulitzer Prize winner?

Komunyakaa touches the round gold rim of his glasses and tells you how: He dreamed himself away.

Dreaming has always been his mode of escape, he says. Perhaps at first it was the seed of the poet beginning to bloom in his spirit. Since life was hard on the outer edges, he started to examine the inner workings of things, to take them apart to see what they were made of. Not mechanical things: "I wasn't interested in machines. I was interested in disassembling and dismembering parts of nature by observation and inquiry."

Later, in Vietnam, he also found a refuge in dreaming, even in the midst of insurmountable horror and chaos.

Back from the war, he dealt with his residual anger and grief by unpacking the emotional baggage he had carried home and pouring it out through poetry. For example, in the poem "We Never Know," the impact of his words stuns the reader almost as surely as the bullet that kills a fellow soldier:

> He danced with tall grass
> for a moment, like he was swaying
> with a woman. Our gun barrels
> glowed white-hot
> when I got to him,
> a blue halo
> of flies had already claimed him.
> I pulled the crumbled photograph
> from his fingers.
> There's no other way
> to say this: I fell in love.
> The morning cleared again,
> except for a distant mortar
> & somewhere choppers taking off.
> I slid the wallet into his pocket
> & turned him over, so he wouldn't be
> kissing the ground.

In 1994, Komunyakaa won the Pulitzer Prize for Poetry and the Kingsley-Tufts Poetry Award for his book *Neon Vernacular,* and this year he is scheduled to be awarded the Hanes Poetry Prize, one of the highest honors the literary world has to offer. His work illustrates the unquenchable curiosity of a man plugging into the very energy of the universe, a man still dissecting and disassembling ideas and images to create poetry with so much strength it seems to have been built of meat, muscle and bone.

Komunyakaa was born in Bogalusa, Louisiana, in 1947, in the sultry humidity and enervating heat of the deep, deep South. His home town is situated on the edge of the Pearl River, its edges defined by steamy swamps and sun-scorched palmettos, scrub oaks, and kudzu. In the town of Bogalusa, oil trucks rumble through streets lined with machine shops, catfish restaurants and crab shacks.

Komunyakaa grew up on the outskirts of town, the oldest son of a finishing carpenter who was filled with a rage so thorough, it alienated him from his six children and chased away his wife. There was a special tension between J. W., the father, and Yusef, the first son, because from the beginning, they had different visions of the world, and each fought the other so that his own view might survive. It was to be years before they made peace with each other. And when they finally did, the father looked at his son and casually asked him to write a poem for him. Yusef, however, could not capture the essence of him until after his death. "There was that kind of realization on his part, that no, Yusef isn't going to work side by side with me, building houses or doing anything of this sort: he is going to write poems.

"I think it was his way of saying, yes, that is all right. It is fine to do whatever you want to do."

In "Songs for My Father," the lines reveal the love/hate relationship of the two and the son's reaction to the physical abuse of his mother:

> If you hit her again, I'll sail through
> That house like a dustdevil.
> Everyone & everything here
> Is turning against you,
>
> . . . .
> I know you'll try to kill me

When it happens. You know
I'm your son & it's bound to happen.
Sometimes I close my eyes till I am
On a sea of falling dogwood blossoms,
But someday this won't work.

Someday, this won't work, he said. Yet, dreaming continued to serve him. At 22 he went to Vietnam as correspondent and editor for *The Southern Cross* and ended up winning the Bronze Star for valor. And finally, he changed the course of his life by seeking an education through the G.I. Bill, a soldier's reward for enduring a tour of duty in purgatory. Komunyakaa earned a B.A. from the University of Colorado, an M.A. from Colorado State, and an M.F.A. from the University of California, Irvine. His shining intellect and dogged persistence pushed him up from the poverty that had eaten away the hearts of many a black man before him, the same poverty that daily gnawed away at his father.

Komunyakaa describes his father as a black Calvinist who believed that work was salvation. "My father was a carpenter and my great-grandfather had been a carpenter, too. My earliest memories of my father are when he worked at the Magazine Lumber Company. I was fascinated with this image. I could look across from my home, less than a half a mile away, and see my father at work. I could see logs piled, not in stacks, but in huge pyramids. My father had a long cable with tongs on the end of it that would grab the logs and take them up in the air.

"He did not read or write, yet he taught himself to be a carpenter. My mother showed him how to write his signature. But he was a very smart man, good with numbers and certain kinds of equations, good in the way he did things. He was very precise, very organized, very meticulous. In fact, watching my father at work is how I learned how to revise my poetry.

"Sometimes," Komunyakaa muses, "fathers and sons have trouble, especially older sons, and I'm the oldest. I think there is competition, because, let's face it, the father serves as instrument of instruction. And for some reason, growing up in America, the competition always has to do with money and position. My father thought that if you had money and property, you had made it. He equated that with salvation, and for him, it was salvation.

"Early on it was quite a violent relationship. And then, all at once, when I was about 12 or 13, the relationship completely changed. There had always been a contest about work, physical labor, because that is what he respected, and then there came a point when I could do more work than he could. That is the point at which we began to become great friends. And it seemed to be my physical strength that precipitated that. For me, it was an arrival. For him, it was a realization." Although the requested poem came too late, Komunyakaa says he sometimes feels his father's presence or sees him in a way that comforts him, and he believes that their relationship has now been mended completely, even after his father's death.

Another way that Komunyakaa escaped the isolation of rural Louisiana in the '40s and '50s was through reading. Although there were few books available, Komunyakaa's mother saw that Yusef had something to read, if only the thin-papered, cheap encyclopedias sold in grocery stores. To feed his hunger for knowledge, she also bought one of the stereoscopes that allow the viewer to see images with three-dimensional depth. Komunyakaa spent hours looking through the lens into a much broader world than he had ever imagined.

"Those pictures really came at me. I kept looking at them over and over. Big caves, shots from other countries, rivers, ocean views. There was a whole chemistry of images." Those images were also important in the birth of his poetry, giving him shapes and forms to apply to the emotions of his exploding artistic awakening.

The pictures in the viewer ignited the fire of the boy's imagination, and with every new image the flames intensified, until one day they blew into a wildfire. That was the day he discovered a meager library across from a small country church and opened a book to a photograph of the black author James Baldwin. For Yusef Komunyakaa, it was a true epiphany.

"This little library run by a church, Mount Mariah Church, was just one room. I just walked in one day after playing baseball and picked up James Baldwin's *Nobody Knows My Name.* It was one of those things that seems meant to be, as if I had been led there. I was quite taken with his photograph. I thought, a writer can look like Baldwin. He looked so typical, as if he could have come from my community. I made a real connection with that photograph, a visual connection. Then I read his words and they were very magical to me. They had a kind of beauty, eloquence."

From that day on, Komunyakaa began reading everything he could find. His appetite was unquenchable. He read all of Baldwin and then he started with other authors. And when he read poetry, his father railed. How could poetry be relevant to the life or the future of a poor black man in Louisiana?

The literature began to make him aware of other things. He began to study the world around him, noticing animals, rituals, sounds of the land, the humming undercurrent of life in nature and the community. In that respect, he was far different from his brothers and sisters. Where they were attuned to working things, Komunyakaa was fascinated with the natural world." I think they were looking at different things than I was. One of my brothers, Arthur, was so intensely interested in machines, he would take clocks apart and put them back together. But it was the soil itself that was really important to me, and the things that grew out of the soil. At that time, my father had a huge garden. It was three acres, but he called it his garden, even though it was more like a little farm. He would plant corn, he would plant potatoes, peanuts, okra, collard greens, black-eyed peas, butterbeans, all these things. He planted what we ate.

"I helped him, of course. He had a couple of cows and some hogs. As a matter of fact, my first successful planting happened because he moved the hog pen. It would be one place for a year, then he would move it somewhere else the next year. I must have been about five years old when I decided to plant pumpkins. I staked out the territory where the hog pen had been and I planted pumpkins. The pumpkins grew huge, huge. I suppose that was my first success, and my father was quite surprised by that."

When Yusef was 10, his mother left home, unable to endure her husband's physical abuse. Although Yusef wrote to her, he continued to grieve over her absence. The children were sent alternatively to live with both sets of grandparents, and although that life offered new worlds to explore, the home was irrevocably broken up.

"My mother ended up in Phoenix," the poet says. "I have a poem about writing to her. It's called "My Father's Love Letters," but that poem is really about me, writing my mother:

> On Fridays he'd open a can of Jax
> After coming home from the mill,
> & ask me to write a letter to my mother
> Who sent postcards of desert flowers
> Taller than men. He would beg,
> Promising to never beat her
> Again. Somehow I was happy
> She had gone, & sometimes wanted
> To slip in a reminder, how Mary Lou
> Williams' "Polka Dot & Moonbeams"
> Never made the swelling go down.
> His carpenter's apron always bulged
> With old nails, a claw hammer
> Looped at his side & extension cords
> Coiled around his feet.
> Words rolled from under the pressure
> Of my ballpoint: Love.
> Baby, Honey, Please.
> We sat in quiet brutality
> Of voltage meters & pipe threaders,
> Lost between sentences . . .
> The gleam of a five-pound wedge
> On the concrete floor
> Pulled a sunset
> Through the doorway of his toolshed.
> I wondered if she laughed
> & held them over a gas burner.
> My father could only sign
> His name, but he'd look at blueprints
> & say how many bricks
> Formed each wall. This man,

Who stole roses & hyacinth
For his yard, would stand there
With eyes closed & fists balled,
Laboring over a simple word, almost
Redeemed by what he tried to say.

"My father remarried, and there was love and care
from my stepmother. But I was always somewhere else,
always thinking of my mother.

"I could only write her. I ended up staying with my
father, but mostly with my grandmothers. I had a very
close relationship with both of them, and in some ways
I am more connected to my grandmothers than to my
parents. It was also a source of information. They would
tell me a lot about history, their own personal lives. My
great-grandmother on my father's side had been a slave,
but she preferred to talk about farming, because that is
what she had then. I remember the one thing she gave
me. She gave me a dog and taught me a great lesson. I
wanted a dog, and she had a huge dog there on her farm,
and she said, 'You can have it. Take it.' Just like that. It
was a country dog. It wasn't used to our cars in the city,
and when I took the dog back to town he lasted for two
or three days before he got hit by a car. The lesson is,
don't take a country dog to town. But the lesson is also
about place. That dog fitted in that particular place, the
farm. I agonized about whether I should tell my great-
grandmother. But in the end, I never could tell her that
the dog got killed.

"I'm lucky for the simple reason that one of my
grandmothers is still alive and that I grew up in an
extended family. My great-grandfather taught me about
farming. He had a huge farm—hundreds of acres. And
when I was 10, right after my father and mother separated,

I went to stay with my great uncle, L. B. McGhee, in a small town called Hackley, outside of Franklinton.

"It was a place where I learned a lot. My great grandfather was a very interesting man—carpenter, brick mason, but a farmer, too. He sent his sons, the sons who wanted to go, to college. They were married to teachers. In fact, my fourth grade teacher was my aunt."

There were a few books at his great-grandfather's house, and also a piano, and Komunyakaa, who is known as a jazz poet, grew up where blues, jazz and gospel poured from the doors and windows in the black community. Exotic sounds hung on the air like clothes on a line.

"The radio," the poet recalls, "was like a shrine, and it was a moment of inquiry for me. I would edge behind the radio and look at the glow of the tubes. That was my first discovery of heat. One could place one's hand there and touch those silver-white tubes, especially when the radio had been going half a day, and it was pretty warm back there. I listened to jazz, blues, gospel—lots of gospel—coming out of New Orleans. I think music has a lot to do with language and it inspired my attraction for language and imagery.".

Another important influence on the poet's language was the Bible. "As a teenager, I read the Bible through, once. At the time I wanted to become a minister. I had a feeling it was something I could really do. It was very strange. As a teenager, I said, 'I can do this, but I have to be prepared,' so I read the Bible through, and I read it through again. I was particularly taken with Revelations because of the images, the rather graphic, horrific images. But also it began to touch my imagination.

"Well, halfway through reading the Bible the second time, I got to this point where I began to look at things happening around me. I was thinking about how churches were so segregated. There were no whites in my church and no blacks in the white church.

"I began to question that. I said, 'Wait, this doesn't make sense to me.' So it really became an exercise in logic. Long before I read Plato or Socrates, it became an exercise of logical construction which caused me to question the whole insti-tution, but I do think there is a spirituality in people. Most people do try to be decent and good. At the same time, I've seen people who were religious and weren't good people.

"I lived in the black community. There was that immense racial division and I learned that the bridge between whites and blacks had to do with work. At one time I had three jobs, another time I had two jobs, and I would venture into the white community only as a worker. In high school I got a job with the Bogalusa Chamber of Commerce, cleaning up the place. Cutting grass—I did that, too. During this time I met a white woman named Williams, from Little Rock. We were able to talk about things in a different way that had never been the case for me as a black person, because there was an immense silence. That's what I mean about silence being political. People just did not talk about certain things. But with this person I was able to talk about education. I hadn't thought about going to college, but she kept telling me, 'You really want to go to college.'

"I remember when it was politically correct for everyone to take segregation for granted. In Bogalusa at this particular time, if a black person was in line at a bank, any white person could step ahead of him, and nothing was said about it."

Komunyakaa's closest childhood friend was a white boy, John Whalen. Neither of them noticed their different colors. "But when school started that friendship was severed. He went one way and I went another way. I remember being heartbroken, and I think he was also heartbroken and mesmerized by this situation. But we were silent. We lived in different worlds, and we never got to see each other again. I don't know where John is today. We grew up with bussing. He was bussed right past my black school on the way to his white school. Baldwin talks about this, about how blacks and whites live in both worlds, but in the South, they still in a way are cousins–kissing cousins with a shared history.

"I remember blacks didn't even talk about it among themselves. My father didn't talk about it. The older generation definitely didn't talk about it. I began to question things early on and I think in my generation a lot of people began to question things. They questioned, but there was no answer.

"When you look at it now, though, you know how much change has happened. It has been huge, but when you talk to young people today, they have no concept about this change, this immense change in our lifetime."

Some of that change was brought on by the war in Vietnam where black men and white men fought and died side by side and color was of no concern. That war shaped Komunyakaa as much as any other single event in his life. When he was drafted in 1968, he sailed through Officer's Candidate School and just as quickly found himself on the front lines with an M-16, a pen and a pad, and told to write war stories as a correspondent for the U.S. Army. "I was on the front line every day," he says. "Every day. I don't have bad dreams about Vietnam, I never did. I did relate to the landscape because the vegetation reminded me of Bogalusa. Maybe that is part of it. I felt quite at home in Vietnam.

"You know, we sort of internalize a place and we carry that place around with us and it becomes a psychological overlay for all the images, all the feelings, the ideas, impulses that we incorporate into our daily lives. Sometimes we go away to get closer to a place. So when I went to Vietnam, I wasn't afraid of the essence of the vegetation. What I mean is that I felt there was a kind of celebration within the context of the landscape, the same kind of celebration that I grew up with, the idea that anything would grow. There was a quality of greenness. I was quite taken with that.

"And I remember I was able to get away from things." One way was through reading. When he left the States, he took two books with him: Hayden Carruth's anthology, *The Voice Great Within Us* and Donald Allen's *The New American Poetry.* He was never without them. The other escape was dreaming himself away, the same device he had used to escape violence as a child. "There was a moment late in the day," he recalls, "when I would go to a certain gully. Elephant grass grew around it and I would watch the medivac helicopters come into this hospital right across the field where they would take the wounded off on stretchers and run them into the hospital.

"This was on the right side. On the left side was the South China Sea. I could see these little round boats, fishing boats. I would try and go there close to twilight.

I did that quite a bit, whenever I could, because on that side you didn't know a war was going on."

During the day there was no time to dream. "As a correspondent I was out at the front every day. One of my closest friends, Andrew Johnson, a boy I grew up with, got killed, and I had other friends who were killed."

Komunyakaa peers out from his formal military portrait with wide eyes and an expectant expression that seems heavy with realization. When he got home, he didn't talk about Vietnam. He threw himself into university studies. "I ended up at the University of Colorado. I remember having an immense amount of energy. I took a lot of classes and finished my degree in five semesters. That's pretty crazy when you think about it. I did a lot of other things as well. I edited the school paper. I edited the literary magazine. I was involved with student government. I was vice president of the black student union. I couldn't understand it. I think Nam did that because I know that many people came back with anxiety. It was a way of dealing with the war. One loses oneself in something else."

"In 1990 I went back to Vietnam with five other American writers who were invited to meet with the Vietnamese Writers' Union. Vietnamese are great readers. It is amazing. You can talk to them about anything in American literature. Many times, especially with the older Vietnamese, they would have read these writers in translation, in French. Certain translations of Jack London or Faulkner or Hemingway have been translated from the French into Vietnamese.

"When I got to Hanoi, the first day or so was agonizing because of memories. And then I began to talk to people. I was taken by the fact that they had been fighting for such a long time. I talked to one man in his forties who said, 'You know, I never experienced my teenage years. What I would like to do is go back and relive those years. As a teenager I was in a war.'

I really identified with that. We were young, too. And they call it the American War.

"Some Vietnamese veterans identify in such an intricate way with American veterans. They really care for American veterans for some reason. I'm still trying to understand that.

"Maybe it comes down to being a survivor. But for me, surviving goes back to Louisiana.

"I think that is part of coping, seeing the beauty in a place and also the terror at the same time. And it also goes back to the rituals observed in nature as a child. You see beauty and terror side by side. That is what poetry is made out of as well, beauty and terror, the alignment that creates tension.

"My investigation as a child, looking at the rituals of birds, looking at the rituals of snakes and alligators in the private lakes, drew a demarcation line between things, a little path I could walk down emotionally, realizing there is beauty on one side and terror on the other side. Sometimes they connect.

"In the last few years I have been trying to go back over the essence of my life. Baldwin says that we have to know what is happening around us in order to know what is happening to us because we are part of everything around us." Komunyakaa's preoccupation with the conjunction of terror and beauty brings him back to the family. "I think it has a lot to do with Americans as dreamers. There is always this great dream to venture out, to be productive, to be successful. They are contradictions."

Unless you are Yusef Komunyakaa, who has put the puzzle of contradictions together in one grand and glorious song.

Excerpt from the poem "Back Then" in *Neon Vernacular*:

I've eaten handfuls of fire
back to the bright sea
of my first breath
riding the hipbone of memory
& saw a wheel of birds
a bridge into the morning
but that was when gold
didn't burn out a man's eyes
before auction blocks
groaned in courtyards
& nearly got the best of me
that was when the spine
of every ebony tree wasn't
a pale woman's easy chair
black earth-mother of us all
crack in the bones & sombre
eyes embedded like beetles
in stoic heartwood
seldom have I needed
to shake a hornet's nest
from the breastplate
fire over the ground
pain tears me to pieces
at the pottery wheel
of each dawn
an antelope leaps
in the heartbeat
of the talking drum

Photo by Fred Brown.

GEORGE GARRETT

"Very few other parts of the country have had the kind of economic and social experience the South had. And basically we are talking about almost 100 years of being frozen and then rapid change after that."

When your daddy is an influential lawyer who can't be swayed by politics or corruption and your uncle is an eccentric screenwriter who drives big Hollywood cars and has access to Al Capone, when your grandfather smokes cigars in church and you grow up in a flat hot country dotted with scrub brush and orange groves, chances are you'll end up being a storyteller like George Garrett. And as storyteller, Garrett is one of the finest in the South.

George Garrett is a man you like to see coming toward you. It's not just the brilliant, ever-present smile or the clean, polished appearance or the pleasant, husky voice. When you see George Garrett you know he is going to tell you a good story—not maybe, not probably—he is definitely going to tell you a good story, and he is definitely going to make you laugh.

This is the public George Garrett—comic, earthy, accessible. On the flip side, you will find the highly serious and intellectual scholar, author of three acclaimed historical novels born through years of serious research. Thus it seems appropriate that the writer's milieu is the historic campus of the University of Virginia in Charlottesville, where Thomas Jefferson's spirit still pervades the pavilions and gardens of the "Academical Village" he planned over 200 years ago. Garrett is the Henry Hoyns Professor of English at UVA, where he heads the MFA program in Creative Writing. He is also a member of the Authors and Writers Guild and has just handed over to Doris Betts the chancellorship of the Fellowship of Southern Writers. He has taught at universities and writers' workshops across the country, mostly in the South, has published stories, poems, and critical essays, edited anthologies, and written screenplays for movies. With all this widespread activity and public investment, he still makes time to serve as mentor to both young and established writers.

His own work has earned him a string of enviable awards, from a Guggenheim in 1974 and the T.S. Eliot Award for creative writing in 1989, to the PEN/Malamud Award for short fiction in 1991. Where does all this ambitious drive originate? From the beginning of his life, Garrett's inordinate energy and enthusiasm were encouraged by a nurturing and privileged childhood in Orlando, Florida, in a family that he describes as "not wealthy, but well-to-do."

In the 1920's, Florida's sparsely settled landscape boasted little more than bushy-headed orange groves and sprawling cattle country, not the mega Disneyesque tourist jungle we know today. Garrett's father, George Palmer Garrett, was an attorney who became not only an authority in Florida legal circles, but a father figure to the fledgling Orlando community.

"I grew up in Orlando, which was then a town of about 20,000 to 25,000 people," Garrett says. "Throughout my childhood there, Orlando was not growing and Florida was not growing. I don't even recognize the place now. It's a million people. A big change took place in World War II when they put in a lot of airfields and brought in more than 50,000 soldiers, doubling the population almost overnight. Prior to that Orlando was a shady country town—mostly farming and citrus. Where we lived was then the southernmost end of town, but now it is right in the middle."

George Garrett was the only boy sandwiched in between two sisters, one seven years older and one seven years younger. An older brother had died in infancy. "It was a happy childhood," Garrett says, and then adds parenthetically, "now that I understand better what an unhappy childhood is. Although in our immediate family, I'm not sure all my cousins had wildly happy childhoods, because they would come to live with us at different times. But we children got wonderful support and nobody ever told us we had to go into business or we had to go out and make money. We were encouraged in whatever direction we wanted to go."

Very early in Garrett's life, the movies became a catalyst for his young imagination, which was ironic, because he later tried his hand at writing screenplays. When Garrett was pre-school age, his older sister and a friend of hers were authorized to take care of him as babysitters. "It was a safe world," says Garrett. "We'd get on a bus and go downtown to the movies. I would be allowed to sit between the girls as long as I behaved. I saw a lot of movies when other kids my age weren't watching them. I had no idea what was going on, and if parts occurred that the girls thought were unfitting for me to see, I had to cover my eyes and wait for them to tell me to take my hands off again."

The movies stimulated Garrett's historical bent, too, even before he learned to read. "I used to dictate stories to my dad when I was four or five years old, and he would carefully write these stories down. I would just rip off something—I was trying to write a huge thing on Richard the Lionhearted. The stories weren't shapely, of course. My mind would wander a lot. Off and on I continued to write as a child, all the way through school.

"We had a game. We used to have a little cottage—a fisherman's shack was what it was, really—over the dunes at New Smyrna Beach. Now it is all built up, but it was quite a lonesome beach in those days. In the evening we had nothing to do other than play the radio, and that was in the car. So we sat around the dining room table and somebody would start a story. We would pass tablets around and you'd put in a paragraph and the next person would put in another. We were always writing."

Religion also played a major role in Garrett's life, and even though Garrett was devout, he still manages to find humor in many episodes that occurred in the church. The family was active in the Episcopal Church in Orlando—St. Luke's Cathedral, and Garrett's father served as the church's legal counselor. Son George was in the choir. On one particular Sunday, when Garrett was five years old, an event occurred that made his family think he might one day become a minister. "The dean of the cathedral—his name was Johnson," Garrett recalls, "was a wonderful guy who was not particularly theological. He was a good tennis player. That was his great interest. He would often interrupt his sermon and start telling stories about things that had happened on the court. Our family had to sit right down front because my dad had a completely deaf side. When he was very young he had been in the Naval Reserve and he was leaning up against a 16-inch cannon when they fired it off. He never could hear on that side again. So he had to sit up close to hear the dean's sermon, right down in the front row. I recall being rather embarrassed about that, but anyway, there we were.

"My grandfather, if he came to church, associated enjoyment with smoking a cigar. So without even thinking about it, if he was really enjoying the sermon, he would light up a cigar, right there in the front row.

"One time, the dean was going through the usual rigmarole. He later said he thought what happened that day was a mystical thing. I jumped up from the front pew and ran up to the pulpit and took hold of the dean's hand and wouldn't let go. So he read his entire sermon holding my hand and then brought me back to the pew. He told my parents he knew that I was destined for the church.

"I have no idea what possessed me. My mother was just horrified, especially because right about that time her father was lighting up his cigar on the other side of the aisle."

Although Garrett went to the Sewanee Military Academy near Chattanooga instead of the seminary, he had another religious experience there, this time with an Episcopal chaplain with a taste for communion wine.

Garrett repeats this incident while smiling his irrepressible smile." By the time I got to Sewanee, " he recalls, "World War II was under way. They were seriously training students at the academy for war. Some of the boys were leaving school and coming back with holes in their heads. When I first got there, the chaplain was looking for volunteers to serve as acolytes right after reveille at 5:30 in the morning, for the 5:45 to 6:15 communion service. But that was also supposed to be the time you cleaned up your room, and nobody wanted to come to communion. So I volunteered to work as the chaplain's acolyte. We usually had maybe three people show up at the chapel for communion. The chaplain, though, would sanctify enough communion wine for the entire cadet corps, huge amounts of it. Then he would serve it really fast. He would give those kids a tongue taste of it and then there would be about a quart or more of communion wine left, very undiluted, and he would say to me, 'You're going to have to help me with this, son.' So we would pass the wine back and forth until it was finished. Consequently, I spent every day at the military academy with a buzz on until around noon. I was a dedicated acolyte. I'd volunteer every time. So, yes, you can say the church had a big influence on me. I thought the church was mystical and sanctified anyway, and with that much wine in me, nothing could harm me. I was unbeatable."

From his father, Garrett learned humility, independence and resourcefulness. Garrett's memory of his father is as a larger-than-life lawyer and part-time cattle rancher who fought for the underdog and usually won. "He was feared," says George the son, his smile broadening into the characteristic Garrett spread. And then he tells the story of how his father's influence shaped his life. "My father had just moved up from Kissimmee. He had worked as a miner and helped to organize in the United Mine Workers. But he got badly hurt and crippled up some, and he was headed to Bolivia to work for an uncle of his down there in the mines when he got as far as Florida. He had some kin there, and he liked it and stayed on. Worked for a law firm. Taught himself the law. Then he actually went to the University of Florida to study law.

"He ended up moving to Orlando. He and his partner, Pat Johnson, in Kissimmee, were the first people to bring Brahamian cattle into Florida, which has now become the essence of the Santa Gertrudis cattle. Then he built this big old frame house that we lived in. I remember it was thought to be a very expensive house in those days because it cost $10,000. It is still there. This was shortly before I was born, so this would have been 1928. It was a two-story house with a nice big attic—not the modern idea of a mansion—it was just a real nice house at the time. I don't know how he made any money to do it because he did so much pro bono work.

"When I was a little older I was able to ask him about it. 'How did you make a living doing this?' I asked. He said he charged well-to-do clients and corporations top fees and they were supporting his pro bono work, that's all. In fact, he did about half his legal work for free.

"It was an unusual position to be in around town, his having that much influence. As I think back on it, he was not a very social person and because of his injuries as a miner, he couldn't play golf, although he did play tennis very well. But he didn't socialize, because he was often representing the downtrodden and poor folks, so we were somewhat at odds with the rest of the community.

"We were relatively well-to-do. Well, yes and no. When the banks went under, we never really lacked for anything, but there were times during the Depression when what we had to eat was what his clients had brought. Once it was one hundred pounds of boiled peanuts. That is all they had to pay with. It was a bartering time. Nobody had any money in those days.

"My father got to be quite a leader locally, not that he was running for office or ever did. But people would come to him for advice on what to do. His rule was to stay out of politics, but be a part of the process."

When the run on the banks took place in the early '30s before the federal government regulated banks, everybody was losing everything they had. Garrett's father went down to the bank where he had his money and said he was going to leave it in there and urged all the people who had gathered out in the street to leave their money in the bank as well. In addition, he promised that he would represent any of them free of charge to get their money back if the bank failed. In fact, while all the other banks went under, that one stayed open because there was not a run on the money. "He never let the bank off the hook, either," Garrett recalls. "He leaned on them until they sooner or later were able to pay everybody back, but his bank did not fail.

"I didn't realize it at the time, but the powerful men in that community were scared to death of my old man, so they were very nice to him. At one point he had whipped the railroad so many times, in so many lawsuits, that they sent a delegation over to our house and offered him a huge retainer to just to promise not to sue the railroads any more. He didn't take it. He said, 'That is more money than I'll ever make, but then what would I do for a good time?' He used to say he didn't drink or smoke because he had an addictive personality, which I can attest to."

George Garrett's father was the perfect role model for the way to live one's life, and another relative—his uncle Oliver Garrett—probably influenced him to be a writer.

After Sewanee, Garrett went to Columbia University for a year, 1948-49, then shifted to Princeton, where he earned a Bachelor's of Arts in English in 1952 and a Master's degree in 1956. Garrett knew by then that his future would be in academics and writing, but he had no inkling when he graduated that he might end up in Hollywood for a while.

Garrett's Uncle Oliver was an award-winning newspaperman in the 1930s and a gifted fiction writer as well. "I didn't see him that much," Garrett recalls. "He was a kind of a godfather who showed up once a year, unannounced, in a big Hollywood automobile with some young, good-looking woman. I always thought he wore funny clothes.

"He got to be a prominent feature writer back in the '20s. Somehow, he got a personal interview with Al Capone when everybody else was looking for him. Right about that time he was invited out to Hollywood to write movies. He ended up writing a great many movies, probably something over 100, including the last screenplay for *Gone With the Wind*. And lots of gangster movies. He was considered an expert on gangsters. He did influence my screenwriting, but not in a conscious way. By the time I got to Los Angeles in the 1960's, he had been dead six or eight years, but a lot of people out there had known him and were very kind to me. David O. Selznick, for instance. He invited me out to his house to a party. Oliver's being out there opened some doors for me." His uncle's association with famous writers also piqued Garrett's interest in literature. "I do remember the time he was hired to write the *Gone With The Wind* script. He was on the way to Key West to visit Ernest Hemingway. Oliver had been an enlisted man in the Army and had spent Christmas 1917 in the trenches. Hemingway was interested in him because of that. Hemingway drove an ambulance, so he wasn't in the trenches. Later they met out in Hollywood and played tennis together and became friends.

"He was on the way to Key West and he got a call at our house from Selznick, asking him to work on the script for *GWTW*. My uncle asked for two things. First, he asked for a whole lot of money. I think he said he would write the script for $250,000, which you can multiply by 10 if you were doing it now. And, second, he insisted on there being no time limit on the length of the script. He was the first writer who had ever done that. Everybody else had broken their backs trying to make that movie come in at 90 minutes, which is the length movies were supposed to be. But Oliver asked for unlimited time. Twenty people wrote scripts for that movie, but Oliver's is the last one before the shooting script."

Garrett later discovered, when reading the memoirs of Salka Viertel, a Hollywood socialite, that when his uncle was living in Malibu, Ms. Viertel was having a big dinner party and the plumbing broke down. Oliver and some of his buddies were sitting on his porch next door drinking whiskey. She enlisted them all to come over and work on the problem.. Among the makeshift repairmen were I. Laurence Stallings, who had lost a leg in the war and wrote *What Price Glory,* and the man who eventually fixed the plumbing problem—-William Faulkner. Oliver also knew Scott Fitzgerald, whom he labeled a "perpetual adolescent."

In 1962 George Garrett himself tried his hand at screenwriting for a year in Los Angeles, but he soon came to that crossroad where a writer decides whether to write serious literature or continue to work on screenplays."There was a point at which there was a serious choice to make and I've never regretted my decision to continue teaching. I wrote about five scripts in a year, three of which were finished. That was unusual. Later I discovered that the worst thing you can possibly do is write a script that is finished. The great screenwriters are the ones whose pictures have never been made. One of mine was a kind of a joke. Three of us were paid $100 each to write a Grade B movie called *Frankenstein Meets the Space Monster* (United Artists, 1966). It has been picked as one of the 100 worst movies of all time.

"I understand and completely identify with Clifford Odette who went out there. All but one of the movies he wrote were all Elvis Presley movies. He wanted to write other stuff, but there is no place for that. I think writing for film is a great art form, but I don't like working in it much."

When he decided to leave California, Garrett says that, in a sense, he drew a line in the sand between where his roots were and where he wanted to be. The roots won.

Although he has spent time away from the South, during a stint in the Army and travels, his native soil has always exerted a strong pull, despite its many problems of racism, poverty, ignorance and intolerance. Like many southerners his age, Garrett remembers the signs on businesses and busses that routed black Americans to the rear or to the "colored" water fountain or to the far, dark balconies in movies houses. Sitting at restaurant counters was also forbidden, and that, perhaps more than any other injustice, represented just how far apart people had drifted. "If you can't break bread together," Garrett says, "then it is little wonder that you cannot understand each other on such complicated issues as race relations and human emotions." While all these inequities were occurring in Garrett's boyhood world, his father was representing black people in court. "He enjoyed a kind of invulnerability because no one would have dared say that he was a 'nigger' lawyer (a derogatory label given to white lawyers who preyed on blacks and took their money without really performing proper legal services). My father, though, wasn't afraid to handle any case and he often worked for free.

"I was aware that there were many forms of injustice and prejudice in the world around, not all of them racial by any means. I remember a hierarchy that always struck me as a class thing rather than a race thing. My father's black clients and others who came calling for any reason always came in the front door. But working people, like a yard man or a solicitor, came to the back door. I did notice that some of my friends made a crack about this.

"We had a black maid, Hattie, who lived at our house. A lot of her family came there and ate meals during the Depression. The kids all played together, black and white kids, and we all ate together because the children in those days did not eat with the grownups. So these were our companions.

"I did know that they went to a separate school. Sometimes they would stay at our house overnight or sometimes Hattie would bring her kids over in the morning because they didn't have enough to eat at their own house. So in the morning we would all ship off to school and we would go one direction and they would go another.

"When you are a child lots of the adult world seems arbitrary. It never occurred to me that it was right or wrong, and it didn't seem to occur to them too much. It was just that we went to this school and they went to that school. It was like obeying every other adult order: do this or do that.

"So I guess the times it hit me the strongest was when Hattie would travel with us. Some of her older kids were living in New York. We would make this big trip to Cape Cod, sometimes in the car, sometimes by train, and once on a boat from Sanford to New York. My dad might make the trip and then go back home. He would deposit us someplace, like my grandfather's farm in North Carolina or his mother's place up in Cape Cod. Hattie traveled with us all the time. I remember as a young child that a couple of times where we were staying in hotels that we suddenly packed up and left because they had been difficult about whether the black maid could stay in the hotel. This was explained to me as something that very low-class, tacky people do,

Talking to Hattie's mother, who had been a slave in her teenage years, also reinforced Garrett's growing realization of the racial injustices that were then rampant in the South.

Although he has written many stories with southern settings, Garrett's three monumental works of historical fiction—*Death of the Fox: A Novel about Raleigh* (Doubleday, 1971), *The Succession: A Novel of Elizabeth and James* (Doubleday, 1983), and *Entered From the Sun* (Doubleday, 1990) are the works that have gathered him the most honor. He has also published books of poetry and he was the writer who James Jones' family picked to write an official biography of the famed author of *From Here To Eternity.*

Writing in the *Dictionary of Literary Biography Yearbook* in 1983, R. H. W. Dillard lauded Garrett's religious faith as well as his writing, both of which, he says, contributed to the success of his historical fiction. "Aside from his talent and intelligence, both prodigious, what enabled George Garrett to write is what enabled Shakespeare or Tolstoy to write their work at the level they did: a religious belief that gives them an awareness of something larger than the passing moment, that gives them awareness of the presence of the eternal in the temporal, of the universe in the particular."

All writers look for recognition in some fashion or another, says Garrett. And writers are particularly vulnerable, he says, in that they must have approval in order to be published, and thus, successful. "Everybody looks for certification, so that you can say at what time you knew you were a writer. I'm sure people have moments of mystical illumination that they can describe when you actually hold a book in your hand and you say, ' Did I do that?'

"In fact you didn't. Some book designer did that. But you hold that in your hand, and when you go back over a lifetime you can see, if you had good luck, that something might have gone one way, and if you had bad luck, it might have gone another way. But that is the best you can do."

What about competition? Especially competition from a writer long dead. Garrett has done a lot of thinking about Faulkner and his impact on southern writers past and present. For one thing, he notes, Faulkner is probably the last Southerner to be chosen for a Nobel Prize. He compares Faulkner's sphere of influence to Shakespeare's in terms of the effect he had on other English writers for the two hundred years following his death. Some great writers—Dryden, for example—said Shakespeare had already done everything. "In a sense that is true of Faulkner as well," Garrett says. "Faulkner burned up a lot of subject matter. The material is as familiar to writers today as it was to him, I guess, but my theory about Faulkner is that he was more of a pioneer than people realize in that no two of his 25 novels are alike. They are alike in tone, but totally different in their construction. So he didn't exploit one way of doing a book. In one sense everybody who comes after owes him, but in a good way, because he presented endless possibilities just at the point in time when the style of the novel may have seemed shut off. All of a sudden, Faulkner says, 'Here are 25 new ways to do it.'

"Faulkner could not have anticipated the particular South we are living in right now. He had some sense of what the clash was, and he wrote books in essence before his own time. He was deeply into the contemporary South. It is a question of attitude, not of tone. You can be dominated and intimidated by that style that he developed. The tone was developed out of basic practical problems, which very few people seem to consider. He was concerned a lot with writing about basically nonverbal people who are smart and sensitive but not very articulate, not educated in a conventional way. The material to do that with is words, got great gobs of words like Jackson Pollack throwing paint at a canvas. It works, but it wouldn't work and it doesn't work for characters who are themselves highly verbal."

For Faulkner and for Garrett and for all other southern writers, what is that indelible and indefinable quality that sets them apart as regional writers? Is it a geographical phenomenon? "I buy that sense of place for writers up to a point," Garrett says. "It is constantly changing. I think that during the long period beginning with the end of the Civil War, the South had only just begun to recover a little bit when the Depression hit. And basically we are talking about almost 100 years of being frozen and then rapid change after that.

"Very few other parts of the country had that experience, that kind of economic and social experience. I was conscious as a child of hearing my father, who grew oranges, saying that it cost more to ship something from Orlando to New York than it did to ship from New York to Orlando, and by a good deal. This was a punitive measure enacted by the federal government right after the Civil War and it had never changed, not during my father's time. One reason southerners became one-crop people in one town or another is that it would be too prohibitively expensive to ship many of the crops. So southerners are conscious of being in a beleaguered area.

"I don't mind being called a Southern writer. I know some writers get very upset because they want to be known as more than a regional writer. My God, the only thing that limits us is our imagination and our writing." He mentions, for example, Eudora Welty and Flannery O'Connor, who are considered mainstream writers although they are still intrinsically southern. Their characters—freaks, white trash, farmers' daughters, dysfunctional families, domineering mothers, saucy blacks— are all alive and well in the South today as well as in southern literature. "And their world is just as real as any one else's," Garrett says.

In an interview in *Contemporary Authors* Garrett says that he has been writing all of his life, but still feels like a beginner "because one is always beginning, always challenged to learn newly. And what one learns is how you should have done the last book, the last story, the last poem. With that knowledge one commences the next and new ones with innocence rather than experience, with hope and faith and no security.

"This is the joy of the enterprise, always to be challenged, at hazard, working and living a quest without ending for as long as I may live. And for as long as I live I want to continue to try my all at doing it all—fiction, poetry, criticism, drama, films. Treating each and every piece of work as first and last."

Excerpt from *The King of Babylon Shall Not Come Against You:*

You look at Florida, even this backwater part of the state, you look at it for a generation, for a decade, for a year or a season, and what you see is change. Everything changing all the time. New people, new faces, even new flora and fauna down in south Florida around Miami. New plants and animals (and probably viruses) from South America, Africa, India.

If you look at Florida it's changing right before your eyes. Like time-lapse photography of corn growing. In that sense maybe it's just an exaggerated version of the whole country. The United States busily (and without regrets) reinventing itself every decade at the least.

Anyway. You look at Florida, you look around yourself at Paradise Springs, and everything you see seems to be changing. You perceive change. And the American mind-set (at least for the time being) is that perception is everything. Not what you see is what you get, but what you see is all there is. And, like God after Creation, we surmise that all this changing is good.

What interests me more than that is what isn't changing and hasn't changed. I would rather consider what we have in common, the living and the dead, all the generations of us. What holds us together and has not changed . . . .

Where is all this going? What am I trying to argue? Just that we, this place and the people in it, can't begin to be known or understood except as a haunted place, a home for old warriors, ghosts and in the flesh, all the same.

Florida is a pretty place, a postcard place, filling up, day after day, with strangers. but then, that was always so.

Even the Seminoles, the oldest people among us, were strangers. What does it mean, "Seminole," in Creek language—"runaway"? "outcast"? We are all runaways and outcasts.

BOOKS BY GEORGE GARRETT:

The Finished Man
Which Ones Are the Enemy?
In the Briar Patch
Do, Lord, Remember Me
A Wreath for Garibaldi
Death of the Fox
The Succession
Poison Pen
Entered from the Sun
The Old Army Game: A Novel and Stories
The King of Babylon Shall Not Come Against You
King of the Mountain
In the Briar Patch
Cold Ground Was My Bed Last Night
The Magic Striptease
An Evening Performance
The Reverend Ghost: Poems
The Sleeping Gypsy and Other Poems
Abraham's Knife and Other Poems
For a Bitter Season: New and Selected Poems
Welcome to the Medicine Show
To Recollect a Cloud of Ghosts:
Christmas in England 1602-1603
Luck's Shining Child
The Collected Poems of George Garrett
Sir Slob and the Princess, a play
Enchanted Ground, a play
James Jones (Biography)
Understanding Mary Lee Settle
Whistling in the Dark (Personal essays)
The Sorrows of Fat City (Criticism)
My Silk Purse and Yours (Criticism)

Photo by Fred Brown.

Photo courtesy of Doris Betts.

DORIS BETTS

"For me, at the heart of a happy childhood lay one such secret, first to overhear as fact, then to see, and now to tell as a story."

If Doris Betts doesn't know you personally, chances are good that she knows your second cousin or an uncle once removed. And if you are introduced to her as a stranger, you walk away feeling as if you have just talked to an old friend. It is all part of the interconnection that links southerners together and underscores the South's regional sense of community.

Like many other southerners, Betts is a toucher, a handholder with a magnetic warmth that draws people to her. On the day you first meet her in her home town, she's wearing a purple jumper, no makeup, no jewelry. Her hair, brown and streaked with gray, is pulled back and fastened at the neck. In her round, girlish face, her huge dark eyes glitter with the humor that dominates most of her writing and speech.

"What did you notice about the courthouse square when you drove into town?" Betts asks. While you're still thinking about the question, she laughs and lets you off easily. "The Civil War statue," she says. "The soldier is looking north. You see a lot of southern towns with the soldier, although now the soldier and the courthouse are still standing here and everything else is out at the mall."

It's true. It's exactly what's happening in hundreds of southern towns these days, including Betts' own town of Pittsboro, North Carolina, which was founded in 1758. Here, about ten miles south of Chapel Hill and a mile away from the Pittsboro Courthouse, the writer lives with her husband in a blue and white gabled Williamsburg style house on an 80-acre farm bought with proceeds from Betts' celebrated novel *Heading West*. The house is comfortable, a perfect writer's house, swept with light from the long windows and cluttered with books, magazines and manuscripts. It's an appropriate setting for Doris Betts, who is herself an easy and comfortable person, a woman who gives you the impression that though it's a serious world we live in, it is not too serious to enjoy. She laughs a lot at herself, and in both everyday life as well as in her writing, she seems to marvel at the resiliency of other people. For example, think of Violet in "The Ugliest Pilgrim." That character is a confirmation of Betts' ability to combine tragedy, humor and compassion.

It is clear that Betts has some concerns that the world she knew as a child is disappearing little by little. Her comment about the mall reinforces that, as does a story she tells you about the death of the last milk cow in the county. It's not just a simple death: it's a symbol of change. "One of the questions I ask my students," she says, is 'Where are you from?' They think that's a terribly southern question. They might have lived in four or five places, they don't have a hometown. But real southerners understand that question immediately. Even if they have lived in four or five places, they know where they are from."

That sense of history is immensely important to Betts and to most other southern writers. They know where their roots are, and they are always strongly connected to the land and the past. Those connections have largely formed their personal philosophies and, ultimately, their writing. The weight of history and its vast network contributes to the southern storytelling lore as well. "For me," she says, "at the heart of a happy childhood lay one such secret, first to overhear as fact, then to see, and now to tell as a story. My grandparents," Betts remembers, "didn't so much *tell* me stories as allow me to sit around and eavesdrop. Mostly they talked to each other. Gossip. I think gossip is at the source of a lot of storytelling in the South. We love gossip, and there are also some stories that are going to get told over and over again, and you remember those. But to gossip you have to have a community that is somehow interconnected. I can go anywhere in North Carolina and somebody says, 'Do you know so-and-so?' or 'Did you ever teach so-and so?' That kind of connection is the southern attempt to link people together." It's a habit, says Betts, that still exists, despite decentralization of towns and families. Long-standing southernisms are comforting—even precious—to this rapidly changing region.

Doris Betts was born on a farm outside of Statesville, North Carolina, in a house with no running water, no electricity, and no telephone. In her stories, Statesville is often called Greenway. Growing up, she lived in town with her parents, both of whom worked in the cotton mill near Highway 64, and both sets of grandparents lived on farms nearby. For a few years, before her younger cousins were born, Betts was the only grandchild. She was doted on by both sets of grandparents, and she spent summers on the farm, which she calls "back out home." This custom, she points out, is a very southern one that has all but vanished now. There is an touch of nostalgia in her voice when she reflects on the loss of that kind of happy experience, because "to the writer, the advantages of this kind of life are that it is a little microcosm. You know the very young and the very old and you know which uncle drinks and which uncle is a real serious Baptist. You learn a lot about different people and yet they are all held within some kind of affection. I think that is the way writers feel about their characters, even their villains. They cut them a little slack. Flannery O'Connor said that in the South we write about freaks because we are still able to recognize them, but that's only real life."

Critics compared Betts to Flannery O'Connor even before she had read a word of O'Connor's work. She says that her affinity with O'Connor, besides using southern settings and delving into religion, stems from the "tensions between the claim and the fact. I don't think of my stories as Gothic. I think they are about real life. I remember some students of mine were coming back from a trip near Salisbury and they were stopped by the sheriff. Telling me the story, they did an imitation of a redneck sheriff and I realized that he was my cousin. 'You're going to have to watch it,' I told them, 'these people are kin to me.' And that is one of the advantages of having grown up in an extended family and being linked to the land."

Betts recalls walking over the farm with her grandfather Bruce Waugh. Although she now realizes that what he worked was a "hardscrabble farm," she didn't know that as a child. "We ate very well. We grew all of our food. We hunted, too. In hard times you would eat squirrel and rabbit. When I look back, I see that we were poor, but I certainly did not feel poor or deprived. It was a 60-acre farm. It had two or three cows, two mules to plow with. My grandfather sold some things he produced, but mostly it was to sustain the family. We made our own milk and butter, still churned, grew vegetables, canned, and dried apples, had chickens and eggs, and sold a few eggs and butter—and milk when the cow was fresh."

Her paternal grandparents were sharecroppers and her father, born out of wedlock and adopted by the then childless Waughs when he was four years old, grew up in the kind of board house where life was elemental and winter whistled in through cracks in the walls. The house had only one heated room, and when Mrs. Waugh became pregnant with the first of four children of her own, resources were stretched and hard times got harder. But even poverty bound families together. "That whole rural community," Betts reflects, "had a lot of social interaction. For example, that's how my parents met—because their parents' farms were joined. We had black neighbors, too, whom I called 'uncle' and 'aunt,' the aunt having been a midwife for the births of all my grandmother's children. When my grandfather died, Grandmother gave the pump organ to Uncle Henley.

"My father ran away from home in tenth grade and joined the Navy. When he came back home he worked first in the cotton mill and most of the rest of his life for the post office. Mother did not work until I was about eleven, when my father had to go to the VA Hospital to have surgery on his back from an injury he got in the service. That's when Mother went to work in the cotton mill. My father had been a weaver and Mother was an inspector, which meant she cut threads."

Both her parents saved to give their daughter the college education they themselves had been deprived of. And for Betts' mother, the sacrifice included loss of hearing because of the constant noise of the mill machinery. But although her mother was the one who saved most of the money, Betts says it was her father who influenced her most as a writer. He was the reader in the family and the one who taught Betts to read before she ever went to school. In her story, "The Spies in the Herb House," which Betts calls "flat autobiography," she says that a symbol of her father's protestations against poverty "stood inside that tall house, a corner bookcase in the shape of an ascending pagoda holding a ten-dollar set of an encyclopedia. A depression encyclopedia, bought in stubbornness, for me . . . .

"Now read these!" he'd say, glowering, although I was only seven at the time. "They cost ten dollars, read them!

"As a child planning to grow up and be a writer," she recollects, "I started on the other end through avid reading to learn from the trivial details of writers' biographies what decisive childhood preparations I should undertake. If Amy Lowell had smoked cigars I planned to try them; it might be worth infections to become Katherine Mansfield or Elizabeth Barrett Browning. . . . Perhaps it is just as well that the details of many writers' lives remained unknown to me and beyond my imagination."

It wasn't the things her father gave her that influenced Betts as a writer, but the places he took her. Not in a car, no. "Poor people didn't have cars. He would take me to see the things that interested him, like how they made ice at the ice plant. Or, the way you bought groceries then was to walk six blocks and buy them and the store would deliver them later with a truck. But in the meantime, if you saw something interesting along the way, you would stop and see it. We did what newspaper reporters do. In fact, what I liked about my job when I later became a reporter was being able to ask questions that were none of my business and get away with it. The job also enabled me to get behind the scenes of all these interesting questions in life."

Betts' desire to "get behind the scenes" led her to a temporary career in journalism. It began with writing a school newspaper column, which then led to part-time work after school and working during the summer at the Statesville *Daily Record* when she was only 13 and later at the *Chapel Hill Weekly* and *News Leader.* It was an ironic twist, because she had learned to read mainly by poring over newspaper comic strips. "My father read to me, too. Oh yes. It was a pull between my mother's choice of Bible stories and what she called my father's "blood and thunder" westerns. I grew up reading Zane Gray and Edgar Rice Burroughs and I still in fact like that kind of reading."

When her family realized she would rather read than eat, that solved every Christmas present. "And they assumed the best books were the biggest books, because you got the most for your money. By the time I was in the second and third grade, I was getting *Ivanhoe,* which I couldn't understand at all.

"I think it was a bit of a surprise to everyone that I was bookish, and everybody thought I would get over it because it was not good for girls. It might distract you from the fact that you should grow up and get married and have children. But they worked very hard to give me the kind of life they had not had. I think they just wanted me to want something different."

One of Betts' greatest influences as a writer was the language of the Bible. "As a child it inspired me, and it still does. The King James version is still the best. It is concrete. It is very seldom abstract. It humanizes things, it uses metaphor and simile. Everything I know about writing I think I learned subconsciously by listening to my parents read the Bible."

That, too, is why Betts came to writing thinking that every story had to have a moral. Although the kind of moral point emphasized in the Bible is out of style now in literature, Betts says she has trouble shaking the need to end a story with a lesson. "If a story feels like a vignette or a sketch, it is hardly worth one's time. Somehow it ought to illuminate or it ought to do more than just give facts." Probably this is why even the briefest of her stories has a thought-provoking epiphany."I have this terrible habit . . . ," Betts said in an interview in *Contemporary Authors,* "of producing an ending that shimmers out past the book and foreshadows something beyond that somebody will notice. And nobody ever does."

But the reader does notice when, for example, at the end of "The Spies in the Herb House," the narrator (Betts as a child) concludes:

> There was so much I understood that day—valor and patriotism, and the nature of the enemy. Even my fear was specific. The war had come to me and I did not have to go to it. I was one with all the innocent victims of history. The German High Command across the sea had taken an interest in my life and in its termination. Oh, do you see that in the days when the spies were in the Herb House the world was still comprehensible to Betty Sue and me?

That "Oh" in her question seems to reflect the passion and frustration Betts the writer feels in her need to communicate the moral point. Perhaps it was her mother's promise to God that underlined the responsibility. When Mary Ellen Freeze, born with a cleft palate, married William Waugh at the age of 19, she pledged that if God gave her a healthy child she would return that child to His service. It didn't take long. A year later, Doris was born. And though she did not become a spokeswoman for God, she has lived both her personal and literary life pondering the moral point of all of life's lessons.

Her growing up was sprinkled with typical childhood fears and confusions as illustrated in "The Herb House"—ghosts, Nazis, death—but it was a thoroughly happy one. Summers in particular seemed idyllic. "Everybody played out in everybody else's yard, staying outside after supper until you were forced to come home. There was always a vacant lot in which you played baseball and football. Statesville was not a mill town, but there was a mill section on the edge of what is now Front Street. The town began with those big, fine houses, and then they got medium sized when you got to my neighborhood and then out closer to Highway 64 you got to another mill town. Behind us were the railroad shacks and the cotton mill and the sawmill. I lived very much on the edge of the industrial part of the county."

Statesville had three elementary schools, and one was clearly designated for children of the mill workers. It had tough students, says Betts, and there was a lot of playground fighting, but she thinks she got a wonderful education because the school was dominated by "old-maid schoolteachers who were determined to make something out of the 'sow's ears.' Her senior English teacher, Miss Josie White, now in her nineties, taught her how to revise her writing, even though Betts says she "did not wish to learn." Miss White believed that punctuation made a tremendous difference, Betts recalls, and "she had you diagraming sentences, another thing that is very much out of style. But to miss the architecture of the sentence means that you don't know why a dangling participle feels like a rag in a bush." Miss White taught Doris Betts so well that she recently sent Betts a batch of personal papers to use in writing her obituary when she dies.

Everyone in the community was so connected then, says Betts, that "There were even times when teachers came to visit in your home. Your mother cleaned up for a whole day or two, and you had to put on a good dress and sit and behave. And the teacher had to have iced tea.

"I didn't live in the mill village, but I was *of* the mill village because that is where my parents worked, and that's where my friends were from. I walked to school on the railroad tracks, not because my parents wanted me to, but because that was more fun. If you followed those tracks a little bit farther, you would be in what in Statesville was called Rabbit Town. In Abbeville it was called Promised Land. The mill there made khaki for the war effort."

The town house she lived in appears in her first novel, *Tall Houses in Winter.* "It is a very old-fashioned house," Betts recalls, "with tunnels of colored glass by the door. When the light hit it a certain way, you had color in the halls. And there was a large staircase with carved banisters. It sounds elegant, but it wasn't, it was just big.

"Behind the entry there were velvet curtains that wound across the hall to close it off, behind which, of course, you could be a performer, you could have a stage out there, up and down the stairs. It was a wonderful place to play, and I will never forget those lights. Across the street was an old mom-and-pop grocery store and beside that was a service station. The man who owned the service station lived in one of the other apartments in our building, and his daughter and I are lifelong friends.

"Most of the houses I have written about have had that same entrance because it is in my head and it was a good place to grow up." Betts says she has noticed the tendency in western writers, too, to write about houses they have lived in and land they have lived on with the same kind of affection as southerners. Maybe, she surmises, that it is because a lot of southerners went through the Cumberland Gap and settled in the West. "So when I'm out West, I feel that I know those people. I don't have that feeling in the Northeast."

There are other fond memories of that house in which her family rented an apartment. When Betts was about eight years old, a different family took ownership. Instead of the expulsion she feared, the new owners, a family of schoolteachers, opened new vistas for Betts. They gave her access to their personal collection of books, introducing the already voracious reader to dozens of new titles. They also gave her piano lessons.

Another heart-wrenching memory associated with that house is Betts' first love, who lived on the opposite side of the street. The two played football together, but the boy was absolutely oblivious to Betts' feelings toward him. "He will probably always be in my mind,"

Betts says, "because his mother died when he was eight or nine years old. That was the first death that I remember. The body was laid out in the parlor. They were not at all wealthy people, and I will never forget: the mother was dressed in a nightgown. It just never occurred to me that people lay down and died and were buried in their nightgowns.

"That woman didn't figure in my writing, but a lot of other dead people in coffins have. I think you use autobiography much less directly than people think. You use the things, you change the memories around. But the facts of the story are what you use to jump off into the pool with. The facts are the least important element."

Another memorable experience was lying in bed in the dark and listening to the radio. Betts says her love of plot and cause and effect and character interaction came from radio. "It freed the imagination more than television does because in television the pictures are already made for you. But when you were listening to radio, you had to make the picture yourself."

Now in Statesville, the old neighborhood is populated by African-Americans, and white owners have moved on to other areas, exemplifying another of the big changes taking place in the South. "I don't think that prejudice affected me directly until high school. My family had never been prejudiced against blacks. Our ancestors had never owned slaves in the past. Goodness, they worked as hard as slaves themselves. Then several things happened: one when I was working in a dress shop with a young black woman my age, who, of course, went to a different school. We became very good friends. I would visit her house and she would visit mine, but neither one of our families liked it. They didn't like our crossing town. It was very nervous-making for them. I also began to see that our lives were going to diverge, and indeed, within two or three years, when I was in college, I saw her on the street and her husband had broken her arm.

"Another instance happened when I was playing piano for a music store. There was a very gifted young black musician who happened to live on the edge of the white neighborhood. He was from a family of excellent musicians. He would come in and play the piano—he was much better than I—and we would play duets. Then he stopped coming. When I saw him on the street, he somehow indicated to me something negative about his sitting at the same piano with a white girl playing music. That was the end of a very nice friendship, and there had been absolutely nothing untoward about it. For that story to have the same kind of ending today would be unthinkable."

An even more unsettling event occurred when Betts had a radio program called "Youth Views the News." High school students would meet at her house with a wire recorder and talk about what was going on in the world. When every other high school in town had participated, Betts invited Morningside High, which was a black school. The radio station was hesitant to run the program, and Betts' mother was uncertain as to whether she wanted black students to come and sit in her living room drinking Coca Cola. But finally she said, "Well, all right," and then the radio station conceded and the program aired. "Before that," says Betts, "I thought it was separate but equal, but then I realized it wasn't. It was a benchmark for me. Up until then, I thought everybody liked things the way they were."

Part of the transformation of southern fiction has to do with the Civil War, she believes. "We got beat. Stories of the Civil War have transmuted to more individual history and family history, county history, local history. I think as a Southern preoccupation, though, it is pretty well gone now, at least among my students. The change also stems from a shift in class. These days you don't have aristocratic plantation writers like Faulkner. You have people who have come out of the beauty shops and the trailer parks. These are plebeian middle class and lower class writers and women writers who never went to war anyway and are not that much interested in traditions of glory and valor."

In an article for *From Life to Art,* Betts observes:

These women grew up reading the large body of serious Southern literature that came out of the period between two world wars, but the youngest ones also grew up under the shadow of another war with guilts of its own and Saigon as its Appomattox, and more extensive lost causes in national racism and environmental filth.

Since Appomattox, too, the age of puberty has dropped from seventeen to thirteen. Near babies know where babies come from now, and their older sisters are off the pedestal and on the pill. . . . The land of cotton is the integrated, urbanized, crowded land of the computer. In the Kmart checkout line, Dilsey's descendants and those from the Compson and Sartoris clans are all wearing jeans.

The usual literary motifs historically classified as "Southern" are being modified by contemporary male and female, black and white, Southern writers: race, religion, nature, concreteness, family, a sense of evil, history, and so on.

The region has changed externally, but many internal traditions remain the same. "Because we are less homogenized and less crowded in the South," she says, "we still have a sense of individuals and we are still very talkative. We still have the storytelling tradition and the Biblical tradition. Oh, yes, I dreamed about leaving the South. I couldn't wait to get out. I wanted to go to Paris and live on the Left Bank. I thought that is what writers had to do. As it happened, I didn't get out of the South until my late 30's or early 40's. That's the way things turned out and I don't regret that now. I value travelling for that perspective. When I was younger, I thought the South was backward, but it is easy to be critical of wherever you are growing up. And here in the South we have traditional values that we have grown up with. You learn what is expected of people in the world. But part of it is also from a religious view of why you are here: you owe something for being here. There is some rent to be paid for your place in the world."

The southern soldier has paid his rent, Black Americans have paid theirs. So have the sharecroppers and the mill workers and the hardscrabble farmers who scratch a life out of the hard-baked clay. Doris Betts will go on writing about them and recognizing and recording their pain and isolation, and their failures, hopes and successes, and her readers can be assured that for every story she writes, there most certainly will be a moral.

Excerpt from in *The Astronomer and Other Stories:*

She could see the row of them working, their backs turned sullenly to the sun, the arms rising and falling almost languidly in the August heat. Things glinted sometimes in their hands; picks or shovels or spattered buckets caught the sun and held it as brightly as little distant mirrors. Occasionally some of them shouted back and forth, for a head would come up, and down the road a second head to listen; and then the second man would do something by reply, nod or wipe his head with a bandanna or go for fresh tar. She couldn't hear them, of course; they were too far away for that. She could just move the edge of blue ruffled curtain in the living room and look down the long brown field to the highway where they had worked all that morning since the school bus had passed.

Their soundlessness made her think of ants moving; she knew they must live and communicate and move toward a purpose (completion of the highway), but they remained to her some distant, strange and very tiny species. Some kind of bug, she thought with distaste, and her white flesh crawled at the thought.

Photo by Fred Brown.

Photo courtesy of Susan Chappell.

FRED CHAPPELL

"Graham Greene said that childhood is a writer's capital. I think I must have overspent mine two or three times now."

In one breath Fred Chappell talks like the home-grown country boy he is—"I sound like Gomer Pyle on a bad day"—and in the next he's quoting Archimedes like the self-made man of letters he has become—"Give me a lever, a place to stand, and I will move the earth."

He's an enigma, a puzzle glued together with down-home wisdom, good ole boy smarts, practical experience, and a classical intellect. He reminds you of a Jackson Pollock painting—bright, wild, sometimes scattered, sometimes experimental and improvisational, reflecting all the involuted and convoluted aspects of his complicated personality. For example, in *The Gaudy Place* you read:

> Consider Arkie.
> (But it breaks your heart.)
> Teacher used to tell him he didn't exist.
> Arkie shook his head angrily. "Yes I do. I do that." Immediately belligerent.

and then you're hearing an entirely different Chappell in *Farewell, I'm Bound to Leave You:*

> The wind had got into the clocks and blown the hours awry. It was an unsteady wind, rising to a wail at the eaves and corners of this big brick house of my grandparents, then subsiding to insistent whispers that rustled inside the room.

But no matter how arcane or arcadian, Chappell is accessible, so accessible, in fact, that having a conversation with him is like walking into one of those old country stores uniquely integral to the rural southern landscape. It's cool in there, and a little bit dark at first, and it's sensual in the respect that you notice everything: You hear the sound of your footsteps on the wood-plank floor, you smell tobacco and peanuts, you see dust motes floating in the smoky sunlight from the window. An old-timer looks you over, motions for you to pull up a cane-bottom chair and then you listen and he talks—about the state of the country, relatives, mules, the weather, the corn crop, how the fishing is this year.

Talking with Chappell is like that. After a conversation with him you begin to consider things you hadn't thought about before. He's grinning at you with that compelling crooked smile that is so thorough it crinkles his eyes. His head is tilted receptively, as if he is really listening to what you have to say, and he motions you to sit down in a comfortable chair in his living room, a room furnished with the trophies of four decades of writing. Chappell no longer smokes, but somehow you feel that he would seem more at ease with a cigarette in his hand. Something to do with all that nervous energy.

Forget the rumpled appearance: Fred Chappell's mind has impeccably sharp corners, an infallibly crisp recall and a vast and fascinating store of facts and memories. He speaks in a clipped North Carolina mountain accent that hopscotches across words and phrases. But his mind is focused, constantly absorbing, measuring, sifting and shifting. Even when he seems to leave you behind intellectually, his insight gives you illuminating flashes into the highly literate world from which he creates. Though once Chappell burned his poetry in adolescent fury and frustration, today his striking images and luminous words burn into his readers' memories. His stories take you there and back again, to places you have known and places you have been, to the South's seedstock, the homeplace.

When Chappell lopes across the room, you can't help noticing the hitch in his step. In a way it seems bound up with his entire psychological makeup. "I wasn't like the other boys I grew up with," he tells you. "I didn't like cars. Never did. Didn't have a driver's license until I was 21 years old." But that's how it happened. An automobile accident. "I was in a car wreck at 15. Me and some of my friends were out riding around one night. I was sitting in the back of the car. My buddy who was driving wrapped it around a telephone pole and wrapped my leg around my neck. I don't remember much about this episode. No one was killed. I was the only one badly injured. It crushed my right hip. I was six weeks in the hospital and six months on crutches." The hip causes him pain these days because the ball-and-socket inserted 50 years ago is wearing down. Chappell eases into a chair, then leans forward into the conversation like a batter at the plate, planted and ready to take a swing. Not an unfriendly swing, just one that will get him involved. You think about the accident and reflect on how it fits into the background of Fred Chappell's youth—part rural farmboy, part mad youth, part restless soul, part unsatisfied artist, and how all those experiences gave him a base to write from.

Chappell lives just off a busy industrial boulevard and the main arteries of bustling Greensboro, North Carolina, where freight trains compete with automobile traffic buzzing around the Greensboro Coliseum Complex. His house is shouldered into an aging neighborhood of small lots and cracking cement sidewalks tilted up by the huge roots of venerable oaks and maples. Inside his brick house is a vast music collection, hundreds of books, handsome handmade furniture and original art and sculpture.

A professor of English at the University of North Carolina's Greensboro campus, Chappell has lived in this house with his wife Susan for almost four decades. He was born in 1936, the son of James Taylor and Anne Davis Chappell, who were school teachers first, and then, as Chappell phrases it, "they decided they would like to eat some time or another and went into the retail furniture business." Their son Fred grew up working on his grandparents' 100-acre farm three miles outside of Canton, and later in the two furniture stores his parents owned. The tenor of many of Chappell's stories and poems reflects that era when the South was just beginning to move away from its agrarian past to a more modern puzzle of interstates, malls and convenience stores. In his introduction to *That's What I Like About the South,* a collection of stories edited by George Garrett and Paul Ruffin (University of South Carolina Press, 1993), Chappell writes:

> The individual recognizes an obligation to transform
> the history, personal or local or cultural, that he or
> she is burdened with. That is why the characters in

Southern fiction can be so loudly violent or so
dreamily passive, why they keep digging at the roots
of situations; they are trying to hammer the circumstances of the past into a future that transcends these
circumstances. When they are overcome by the enor-
mousness of the task, they may retreat into themselves and dream dreams and swoon with visions. Or
they may attempt, in some overwhelming bafflement
of emotion, to lay forcible hands upon events and
wrench them into a pattern that gives expression to a
personal destiny.

Does Chappell consider himself a "southern"
writer? Absolutely. He says, in the same introduction,

The Southern writer is entranced by Southern cultural history because it is the only story there is. Once
upon a time things were the way they were supposed
to be. Then something happened. Since that point,
things have never been the same. Since that point,
since that single enormous event occurred, we are not
the same people we were before, and our children
will have to be different from all the children who
lived before our time. Not even the land is the same
as it was before, and it records the evidence of that
change and our subsequent sorrowful history. We in-
habit a fallen world where blind ignorance has replaced our early succulent innocence. The
Southerner's history, whether cultural or personal,
contains but one large controlling incident: betrayal.

The fact that the South lost both its people and its
pride in the Civil War inflicted wounds on southerners
that have not thoroughly healed over a hundred years'
time. "My grandmother would tell stories about her
childhood and about her mother," Chappell recalls. "It
was a common topic, but it ended at the Civil War. None

of them would talk much about the Civil War for some reason. They just didn't do it. My great-grandfather Chappell lost a leg at Fredericksburg. My great-grandmother had been robbed on her farm by Union soldiers. I think they stopped at the Civil War because that is as far back as they knew. If they knew more they would have told it. Those would have been good stories."

But for a boy growing up in the South there were plenty of good stories to be found in other places. "Graham Greene said that childhood is a writer's capital," Chappell says. "I think I must have overspent mine two or three times by now. Nevertheless, those are some of my most vivid memories and the ones most resonant to me. It seems to me, and I'm sure this is prejudice: that people were more colorful back in the olden days, especially in rural situations where character had more room to develop its idiosyncracies than it does when people have to live closer together. And you don't have the time it takes to develop a very individual interest and waywardness, so for that reason I enjoyed very much writing about that kind of material and the area I grew up in.

"One of the things that I remember most vividly from being a child is the stores. I had a bicycle and I'd ride to the store to get a Coke, or something like that. There would be some older gentlemen sitting there and every now and then one of them would say, 'Sit down here and talk to me, boy. I'm waiting for my buddies to come.' They just expected you to keep them company and talk to them until someone showed up they really wanted to talk to. You did that. Or you just sat off and listened to them jaw at each other. You heard all kind of things.

"I have never thought of that as being particular regional. I just thought that is what the older folks did then, I think, when they had more leisure time. People still do that, I just don't see it as much as I used to. Older people like to talk and younger people like to listen to them, because older people have more stories. And one of the things that made growing up a little bit difficult was that they had all the good stories and you didn't have any good ones to tell. So when they asked you to talk to them, you always felt a little short-handed. You were just fresh out. But they would encourage you. They always wanted you to speak up for yourself.

"They liked for you to tell them about yourself and look them in the eye when you did it. And they liked it if you knew who your folks were. If you knew that so-and-so was your uncle or not. If you knew where your grandparents came from. They liked for you to know that.

"They would say, 'Now ain't you Uncle James Forthwright's little nephew? And where is he now? Didn't he move off Smathers Hill over there? I hear he is down at Frog Level now. Is that the way it is?

"Well, they know more about it than you do. But they would send you through the catechism anyway. They were just checking up on you."

Both Chappell's parents and his grandmother were extremely influential in his formative years. "I grew up in two houses. I grew up in my parents' two-story white wooden house which was about 200 yards down a dirt road from a hilltop where my grandparents' larger brick house was. My grandfather built both of the houses. The one he built for himself and my grandmother still stands.

"His houses are the sturdiest houses. He would pour a concrete wall six inches thick. Base moldings were solid oak, inch and half, two inches thick. I've seen an electric drill just tear up, burn out, trying to get through it.

"Their house was cool, dark. There were about a dozen tall black oak trees. It was always kind of mysterious and interesting to me. But I liked our house, too, which was a very nice bungalow with an upstairs on it."

Chappell's emergence as a writer began in the fourth grade. Before that, he had been reading long before he ever went to school."I can remember in the fourth grade we wrote a poem and in the sixth grade we wrote a poem. And then when I was 12 or 13 I started writing a lot of poetry. I have no idea why. It was out of my own compulsion. I never stopped writing. Poetry and short stories. I knew then that is what I wanted to do. When I was very young, 12 or 13, 14, John Steinbeck and Ray Bradbury were very important to me. When I was 16 or 17, Thomas Mann and Tolstoy became important to me. This set the stage. A Latin teacher, Mrs. Kellett, was very encouraging. Not in writing English poetry, but just in learning Latin. She was a very good teacher and made me feel enthusiastic about literature. I had a high school teacher—Mrs. Tucker—who showed me that others could be excited about books." In *An Apple for My Teacher* (Louis Rubin, editor, Algonquin Books of Chapel Hill, 1993), Chappell says, "I haven't forgotten the story of her becoming so absorbed in Dick-ens by lamplight that the room filled with smoke and she never noticed." She knew Chappell was interested in writing and she wanted to direct his interest a little, "But," he says, "by this time I was sort of cranky and had my own agenda. This was in my senior year.

"My teachers preferred Victorian poets—Browning and people like that, and I liked W.H. Auden and T.S. Eliot, real modern types. And Whitman. I was real big on Whitman."

Chappell's hometown of Canton is still a papermill town and still has a population of 5,000, about the same as when he was a boy. Champion Paper and Fiber Company located one of its factories there years ago, and it is still in operation.

As a youngster, Chappell worked on his grandparents' farm when he wasn't in one of the furniture stores. "There isn't anything easy about farm work," he recalls. "It is work. That is what I spent most of my time doing. I never resented the work except when I wanted to do something else, like homework. You just kind of took it for granted that work was something you did. I would get up every morning about 5:30 a.m.—milk cows, feed the livestock, pigs and horses. Then we would do what we call pour up the milk. We would run it through spring mountain coolers.

"Then I would go to school."

The Chappells were Huguenots who came to North Carolina and immediately became landowners. His father's family located in Candor on a large farm where they grew peaches, pecans and apples. His mother's family bought land when they moved from Madison County to Haywood County. His grandparents' farm was what he calls "just an all-around, general truck farm of corn, tobacco, hay, truck cut produce. My grandmother and I would take some of it over the hill into Canton and sell to local grocery stores. Or sometimes I would go with my father on Saturday and we would sell produce at the open-air market in Asheville."

These were World War II years in the hills of Appalachia, where times had always been hard, and in those days the region had not yet fully recovered from the fallout of the Great Depression. Better times were coming, but they were to carry an unbelievable price tag. "You spent your evenings staring at the radio," Chappell says, "listening to terrible things happening overseas. I would pass houses on my way home from school with Gold Stars hanging in their windows, and all the young men that had played football the year before were off in the Army.

"It was very difficult to get certain things, like sugar. Gasoline, though—farmers got a better gasoline ration than other people because for them it was a necessity, but there were ordinary shortages. Tires were very hard to come by. Me, I didn't know what they were talking about. I was just eight years old."

The deprivation was endurable: The worst hurt was the boys who lost their lives. "Sure, we knew lots of the boys who didn't come back. It was a tough time. We were just coming out of the Depression and this war. People were tough, cheerful, determined, but not happy. It was the worst of times. There hasn't been a time that hard since—not now, not ever. Not the Vietnam War, not the Korean War. It was the hardest time there (in that region) since the Civil War."

During those years, the family was central. Everywhere Chappell looked, it was the same: families hanging onto the land and each other.

"I worked with my family all day. If my father wasn't teaching, he was working. If my mother wasn't teaching, she was working. My grandmother was always working. We worked together, we ate together. Got up at the same time together. It was a life. When my parents had school activity at night, they would carry me along. I would go to PTA meetings, basketball games (my father was basketball coach for a while). I was even a mascot for one senior class.

"We had to go visit the parents of young men who had been killed in the war. They had decided to enlist without finishing high school. There were five or six. This was over a two-three year period. Once or twice, my father had to go break the news because the people were so isolated. He was at a place where they had no telephones, so he had to drive back in the hills and tell people what happened."

The family was important also because of the subtle social distinctions between the town boys and the farm boys. "Guys who grew up on farms were distinguished from the town kids," says Chappell. "The town boys were more sophisticated and had more money. You get spending money if you work for a paper company. On a farm you don't have ready money a lot, but I guess you have more security. That little bit of economic difference made a lot of difference in the way you grew up."

Chappell says that working closely with his grandmother, Anne Mae Davis, was a highly influential factor in his childhood. "I was her pain staver," he says, laughing. But he felt her pain as well. In his poem, "My Grandmother Washes Her Feet," he writes: "I see her still, unsteadily riding the edge/Of the clawfoot tub, mumbling to her feet/Musing bloodrust water about her ankles/Cotton skirt pulled up, displaying bony/Bruised patchy calves that would make you weep."

"During my most formative years I spent most of my time with my grandmother, since both my parents worked. She directed my farm labor and more or less looked after me. But we all worked together. My mother was a little more demanding than my father. Mother was

Ann Davis Chappell. Father was J.T. (James Taylor). He was easygoing, a funny gentleman. Lots of humor, lots of tolerance, lots of understanding.

"My mother was a very bright, swift person. But she was a little short on patience. She liked to rub people the wrong way. That was her hobby. So she gave me and my one sister an interesting upbringing.

"She was a kind of negative influence most of the time. She tried to throw cold water on your enthusiasm, direct your energies—whichever way they were headed—some other way. Partly because she thought it was constructive, partly because she enjoyed doing it.

"My grandmother was very religious. My mother was very pietistic. The church I went to was very pietistic. The First Methodist Church in Canton. They made me go to Sunday school and church. All that stuff. By the time I was 13, I was a raging atheist. I would go to choir practice on Wednesday nights because that was the only place you could meet girls. I settled down a little bit later and became an agnostic when I was 15. Now I think of myself as a religious person, but no church. I have no interest in organized religion. None whatsoever. I am interested in theology. I read the Bible and have my own ideas about it. I got that guilt stuff from my mother. The only guilt I feel is from stuff I know I have done. God knows, there is plenty of that. I feel guilty when it is appropriate to feel guilty.

"I did not go to revivals when I was growing up. I think my grandfather did sometimes, but my grandmother and everybody else didn't like them much because they took away from the regular church."

Flannery O'Connor said that we write about freaks in the South because we are still able to recognize them.

According to Chappell, there were lots of freaks in Canton. "We were surrounded by madness," he recalls. "Every strange neighbor you can think of. You either put up with him or argued with him or you ignored him. Actually most people did all three." But when he went off to Duke University, it was his own character he had to tame. In *An Apple for My Teacher,* Chappell talks about his first meeting with Reynolds Price, who was then editor of *The Archive,* the oldest college literary magazine in the United States. After consuming a quantity of beer and cooking sherry, Chappell and poet James Applewhite paid a visit to Price's room, planning to impress the upperclassman with their literary expertise, but Price, he says, was "invulnerable. It was clear he had actually read the stuff he talked about." Chappell was so impressed that Price became his role model and friend. "There seemed to be a tacit agreement that I was to be intense and wild and experimental, while he was to be traditional, Olympian and successful."

After graduate school Chappell moved to Greensboro, N.C., in 1964 and began teaching English literature and writing poems, short stories and novels. It was then that he began putting together the discrete images he called up from his boyhood, weaving together the threads of his unique southern tapestry. In many of his stories, the scene has been set at his grandmother's farm for that solid sense of place. "I use my grandfolks' house a lot in stories. And sometimes I will use my parents' house. The reason is that I like to feel at home in a place when I write. And those are familiar places. But I would use any setting that I can remember real well, or go look at and use. I like to feel at home in my head. I like to locate my characters in some place that I'm familiar with, that's not made up, so that they are not just floating."

But Chappell wasn't happy with everything that was going on in the South. He had grown up with segregation of the races, and when he was a child he believed that that was the way things were. But slowly he came to realize the inequities of the system. "There were almost no blacks in Canton," he recalls, "but there was lots of prejudice. I don't know why. We didn't know that many black people. There was a black high school in Canton, but not many black people. In fact, I only knew one black family—Jim Love's. Wonderful people.

"I was against segregation. That caused a little friction between me and my folks, a lot of friction between me and some of my schoolmates. But not all of them. And although my folks didn't believe in integration in the beginning, they came around. I hated prejudice. And one of the things that I had against organized religion is that it promulgated it as far I could tell. I don't think this was true as an official policy of any of the churches, but you heard enough of it.

"When I was 13 or 14 I realized this was wrong morally. I read stories of Erskine Caldwell, and Ray Bradbury had a few stories (about segregation) and John Steinbeck's *Pastures of Heaven*. I read Lillian Smith's *Strange Fruit* at that time. It came out in *Liberty* magazine. I realized some of the injustice of the situation, even though the only segregation I ever saw was at my high school and in the theater we had in town, where black people had to sit way up high in the back.

"I didn't see much of it until I would visit my folks down in Candor in the middle part of the state where there were lots of black people. At that time when I first saw the signs (separating black and white) I didn't know what they meant. I don't think it registered with me. Later on when I remembered them, I was upset about them."

Another battle that Chappell had to fight was his own struggle with alcohol. "Drinking had an effect on my writing many years running. It slowed it down, made it more difficult to do. It made personal relationships harder and ate up writing time. There was a time I drank all day. I would write unevenly. Alcohol is the bane of writers. Yes, it sure is. I don't know why. There is probably some genetic reason. In my case, it bore on writing in two ways. One is that writing is like jumping off a bridge and hoping you land without getting killed. And I think it's the terror of the vocation and the responsibilities: You don't want to write badly for any number of reasons. So drinking is an easy gateway to impulsive behavior, an impulsive thought, a way into the unconscious mind. It is not a good gateway, it is a corrupted one, but it is an easy means and it is very seductive, especially for poets. It is an easy way to stick your hand in the bottom of your mind. Unfortunately, it is not very reliable, and for long periods of time it is deleterious.

"The other reason writers drink is out of despair, because whatever you do falls so far short of what you intended. Drinking sometimes is a way to forget. But mostly for me it was just to have a lot of fun and I'd keep on even after I wasn't having any fun." Now Chappell drinks only a moderate amount of wine.

And for most, if not all, southern writers, there is the shadow of William Faulkner. If you write and live in the South, Chappell says, there is no way around it: At some point, you must confront Faulkner, who gobbled up a great deal of prose real estate in his career. "When I first began publishing novels, I thought a great deal about Faulkner. Now I only think about him when I'm reading him and I haven't read him in a long time. I think he was a wonderful writer, but I have no occasion now to pick him up and read him. Still, I can't imagine a southern writer now who is not aware of Faulkner. I can't imagine a southern writer, black, white, immigrant or whatever, who doesn't know that Faulkner exists and is out there lurking on the horizon. For some of them he makes up the horizon. Edgar Allan Poe is another one. And for some people Tennessee Williams would be included, but not for me."

There was a time before he went to college that Chappell thought about leaving the South. For one thing, he thought it was what you had to do as a writer—be like Hemingway. Leave home. See the world. Write about foreign countries and expatriates.

"I thought I would write a lot of stories and novels and screenplays and get rich in a hurry and move to New York, have a penthouse with movie starlets—hot and cold running movie starlets—then I would go to Europe, and Papa Hemingway and I would shoot some lines.

"But as soon as I got to be 16 I had no ambition to move from the South. It suits me. I don't mean the South suits me. I don't agree with a lot of things that the South espouses, or used to espouse, but I don't see any other place that is any better.

"All writing is regional. It takes place somewhere. It either takes place in a real place you know or it takes place in someplace where you have had to imagine it. For some people that is a very powerful place, the imagined place.

"What was it that Archimedes said?" Chappell asks. "'Give me a lever, a place to stand, and I will move the earth.' Well, writing is my lever, the South is where I stand, and I have ambition to move the earth." But being a writer in the South, he says, is something on the order of being the village oddity. It's like the family that everyone talks about, but respects for their eccentricities.

"The South," he says, "has had a gracious plenty of writers who have altered the literary landscape: Faulkner, Welty, Wolfe, Lee Smith. So there must be some special something in the South that breeds writers. I think it is the relative newness of literacy in the South. I think that when a people or a region gets to be second-generation or third-generation literate, there is some excitement in books and an excitement about writing, excitement about expressing things that you haven't seen expressed before. There is something glamorous about writing, about books, that is not that way to people who have lived in a literate society for quite a long time.

"If you write books in the South, people won't talk about it to you, or mention it, but you are an object of interest to them. If you write books in New York City you are just another guy who writes books. But in the South you are still a little out of the ordinary, a little bit exotic.

"I think to be tagged a southern writer is inevitable. If you were born in the South and grew up in the South and you are interested in what's around you, then you write about southern things." And Fred Chappell has written well about things southern. He has won nearly all the major prizes his state awards for literature, including the Walter Raleigh Prize. And just last December, he picked up a prestigious prize for poetry presented by the *Sewanee Review.* The Aiken Taylor

Award in Modern American Poetry was one more notable recognition in the long writing career that is finally bringing him the attention he has long deserved.

Fred Chappell sits in his upstairs office at home. His writing desk is pushed against a wall and on top of the desk sit a yellow legal pad and a pen. Chappell always writes his first several drafts in longhand, then types out the final draft. The pad and the pen connect him to his work, he claims. "When I started, that is what I had. There wasn't anything else. I just got to trusting to it over four decades of writing. I wouldn't want to change. For me there is a physical involvement in doing this— pressing my hand on the words themselves, which I miss when every once in a while I have to type some- thing out, or when I have to use computers because I'm in a hurry. But I miss the contact. I like to write it out in longhand and then go over it in longhand.

"I keep my hand on the words to pin them down."

The words won't fly away, though. They belong to Fred Chappell and his inimitable style—country boy gone to town—intellectually, that is. Otherwise, he is at home in Greensboro, in North Carolina, in the South, close to the place where he grew up, close to the roots his ancestors put down. His southern accent? To most listeners, that's just a form of regional music that is tran- scended by the words, the rhythm and the syntax of this writer's impeccably elegant poetry and prose. And while he's reading, yeah—he does it. Sometimes Fred Chappell actually manages to move the world.

Excerpt from *Farewell, I'm Bound to Leave You:*

It seemed that my mother told me she had a number of duty calls to pay and asked if I would like to accompany her and it seemed that I was younger than I actually was and said yes and we set out westward toward Hardison County in the old wooden station wagon we used to own and not in the new green Chevrolet sedan. It seemed that we were soon off the main highway, following rattling gravel roads squirming between mountains taller and bluer than any I remember. My mother was wearing a smart linen dress and white gloves and white shoes and kept her gaze on the road, which went continually bright and dark with tree shadow. It was like she was not looking out a windshield but peering into something, a dim corner or a deep well.

"We must pay our respects," she told me. "First to the River Woman, who lives in the grassy bottom acres by the Little Tennessee. Then we must visit the Cloud Woman and the Fire Woman. The Moon Woman lives in a cave on the far side of Ember Mountain; I hear she has been ailing and has had doctors in, so we mustn't stay long, but we have to make our call. If Aunt Priddy is home, we will stop by for tea but then must travel on to see the Deer Woman and the Happiest Woman. But I am most particularly anxious for you to meet the Wind Woman. Do you know why?"

"No, ma'am."

"Well, I saw the other day that you were writing poetry in one of your notebooks. I don't know what you were writing about, but if you ever take a notion to write about our part of the earth, about the trees and hills and streams, about the animals and our friends and neighbors who live in the mountains, then you must meet the Wind Woman, for you'll never write a purposeful word till you do."

. . . She looked away. "I used to write poems. they were about the affections of my heart. My heart was always selfish, but my head has been clear. . . . I wrote them down in pokeberry juice and oak-gall ink. I wrote out the words with many a flourish on the petals of mallow and dogwood petals and morning glory. Then I gathered them all up in a great bedsheet and walked down to the iron bridge over the Pigeon River with them slung on my back. I emptied them out onto the waters. I can still see them floating away in the air like butterflies and then settling on the river in a sunny glistening and floating away down to the boiling rapids. It was a pretty sight, believe me."

. . .This time when she looked at me, shadows from inside her mind rippled over her face like furls in a breeze-raked silk banner. "Excuse me," she said, and pulled over to the side of the road and got out of the station wagon and wept.

Photo by Fred Brown.

Jayne Ann Phillips, seated front. Photo courtesy Jayne Anne Phillips.

JAYNE ANNE PHILLIPS

"The writer somehow becomes responsible for the family story, or the story the family won't tell, and telling it is a labor of love and a compulsion deep enough to last a lifetime."

Jayne Anne Phillips can remember the very day she vowed to travel as far from Buckhannon, West Virginia, as possible. She was eight years old, and the year was 1960. Sitting on the veranda behind the house her father built, she looked out over the rural landscape—a stream, fields and a range of hills she thought of then as mountains. "I was wondering," she says, "just how far I would go from that exact place. It wasn't so much that I wanted to leave, because in fact I was very involved in it and invested in it and soaking it all up. But I was aware from the beginning that I wanted to go everywhere."

Even at that early age, she equated leaving not with money or success, but with independence. "I knew from the time I was very young that I would never change my name, that whatever I did would be associated with my name. I think that had to do with the female legacy that women in the family had not somehow become what they might have become, or owned the power they might have owned."

Phillips changed all that with her solo cross-country trips beginning at age 18 and with the publication of her first book, *Black Tickets*. At age 26, she became an instant celebrity in the literary world , and her subsequent work has only enhanced her reputation. In life, as in literature, Jayne Anne Phillips pulls no punches. Her honest portrayals of characters from the dark side of American society are just as loving and acute as those of the middle-class sisters Lenny and Alma in *Shelter.* Some were shocked by the characters in *Black Tickets*—addicts, prostitutes, drifters—characters Raymond Carver called "the disenfranchised—men and women light-years away from the American dream." But the *Cleveland Plain Dealer* maintained that those misbegotten wanderers were somehow transformed by the poetic vision of the author. Whatever the social class of Phillips' characters, she is able to portray their innate dignity with an empathy that transfers directly to the reader. As a storyteller she is like a chameleon, sliding into each new identity with subtle ease and absolute authority.

Phillips is a stunningly beautiful woman with long dark hair and a gaze as direct as an x-ray. She is married to a physician and has two sons, and beyond that she is hesitant to divulge information about her personal life. But through a cross-section of her writing, the reader emerges with a strong sense of her complicated personality and discovers that her understructure is supported by a rigid backbone and an unrelenting sense of honesty.

Born in 1952, Phillips spent the first 18 years of her life in the town where she was born, the town that served as the setting for her acclaimed novel *Machine Dreams*. Buckhannon was the county seat, a town of about 8,000 people at the time she was growing up. It is about two hours from the Pennsylvania line and on the borderline between North and South. The geographical and political identity of the town has been debated ever since West Virginia separated from Virginia to protest the institution of slavery. Phillips says that when she was researching her family history she found a story of a relative whose sons were fighting for the North, while she, the mother, was spying for the South. "That gives you a sense of how divided people could be,"she says. In many ways, though, the state remained southern rather than northern, and Jayne Anne Phillips has been categorically classified as a southern writer, compared to Faulkner and Cormac McCarthy. Those who liken her to Eudora Welty and Flannery O'Connor probably make the comparison because of her substantial investment in place. But although there is indeed a southern flavor to her work, her themes are patently universal.

The town of Buckhannon suffered the same fate of most West Virginia towns. It was exploited by outsiders first for timber and then coal. When the deep mines were exhausted, strip mining decimated the natural resources of certain areas, and local people were left with little or no money and few resources. Still, the physical isolation of the place and the common problems created a sense of community, and Phillips says she felt insulated and secure growing up there. Since Buckhannon was a coal mining area, mining or support services for the town were the only available jobs. There were also a couple of factories that have now closed down. One large consolidated high school pulled in students from all over the county, and West Virginia Wesleyan College, a Methodist school that figured in *Machine Dreams,* is also located there. Despite its small population, Buckhannon was the biggest town in the county and Phillips recalls it as thriving when she was growing up. "On Saturdays it was so crowded you couldn't drive on Main Street. All the people from the county came in to do their shopping and all the stores were open. Businesses usually stayed in the same family. There was a men's clothing store and two or three restaurants that the same people had been running for 30 years, real restaurants, real lunch counters—and a huge five-and-dime. Now a lot of those places are gone and the town has become a reduced version of America that has to do with instant media and chain restaurants."

Phillips describes her family and the town of Buckhannon as solidly middle class. "People who lived in town," she says, "were a little better off than the people who lived out in the country, but middle class meant something different then. There were no private schools, nobody vacationed in Europe. And they didn't want to."

Phillips' father was a contractor who worked for the State Road Commission, an office that supervised the construction of sidewalks and streets. "He was born in 1910, and he had done a number of other jobs before that. He didn't marry until he was 38—he was 15 years older than my mother—and I think he started to college but never finished."

Her mother was a school teacher who taught first grade for years and later became an administrator.

Phillips had two brothers—one older and one younger, but their interests were vastly different. "My mother always encouraged us to read, but she'd give the boys books and they'd look at them and throw them down, so I was just the one it took with. But even though my mother was a reading teacher, she didn't really read literature. None of my family did. My father used to read books that were considered contraband. He kept them in the bathroom cabinet where towels were stored, high up next to the ceiling. They were mostly thrillers and spy novels with racy covers. I used to go through those books on the sly, and once I found *Rabbit Run.* It was the mass-market edition and I remember a woman in spike heels on the cover. I read it in secret when I was about nine.

"At about the same time, I read a series of leather-bound Galsworthy novels that my grandmother had owned. My mother kept them in what we called the secretary in the living room—a massive oak piece of furniture that my grandfather, who was a furniture maker, might have made, but it was probably much older than that. The other books I read were really just books for kids. I went to a small-town school, and I really didn't start reading contemporary writers until I left high school. I did read *Huckleberry Finn* and the few books that were assigned in classes, but I didn't know anybody who was literally going to tell me to read, and I don't remember any teachers who were influential in that way. For example, they would have thought Faulkner was inappropriate. It wasn't really until I left town that I began reading everything."

Phillips' work has received shimmering reviews— "mesmerizing, sensual, lustrous, exquisite." She believes that writing is both a gift and a responsibility. "I think the person who becomes a writer does so because of genetics. I think we are born that kind of person, but it is also a question of family politics and birth order, the unresolved dilemmas inside the family and inside the parents' marriage. I've also observed that most writers have a particularly close unboundaried relationship with one parent, usually the mother. And people often become artists for reasons that go beyond ego. In a way, it's not something you choose to do, but something you evolve into. The writer somehow becomes responsible for the family story, or the story the family won't tell, and telling it is a labor of love and a compulsion deep enough to last a lifetime.

"Writing is really not a career and not exactly a choice. I think it has to do with a sense of being the confidante of one of the parents and somehow carrying the burden of loss that exists inside the family."

Phillips accepted the burden of being the family chronicler when she inherited the family stories from her mother, who came from a line of strong female figures. Her mother had grown up practically like an only child because three siblings had died close to her own birth. The other two living children in the family were 10 and 12 years older. During the time she was growing up, the family was in reduced circumstances and she was living alone with her mother. So Phillips inherited the stories of the women in the family. "Since there was little communication between my parents," she says, "there was nowhere to take those stories but to me. I think in families where there is one daughter, particularly in areas of the country where sexual roles are so narrow, the bond between the mother and daughter is very, very strong. It wasn't characteristic for women to confide their histories in a son, although they did it if they had only sons. In that case they would pick the one who was the best listener. I've talked to so many male writers who had a kind of particularly close, although possibly troubled, relationship with their mothers. It doesn't necessarily mean that it's a relationship with no tension. Quite the contrary." The thwarted needs or desires or ambitions of the mother may not be articulated by the writer the way the mother intended, says Phillips. They may in fact be expressed in ways the mother finds disturbing or confounding.

That was the case when *Black Tickets* came out. Phillips' mother was shocked, and, Phillips says, "just not on my wave length." She wanted to know why her daughter had to use four-letter words and write about people on the edge of society who experimented with drugs and illicit sex. But a review by Carol Rumens in the Times Literary Supplement praised the book and said of Phillips: "She takes street slang all the way to poetry and back."

Before this first widely published expression of Phillips' observations on life outside Buckhannon, her stories had been published in small magazines and journals, literary publications her parents were not likely to see. And although they knew she was winning poetry prizes at college, the poems were less direct than the fiction, so the impact of *Black Tickets* seemed especially volatile.

"That part of it was hard," Phillips recalls. "But they were both very generous. My father's concern was whether I would ever make a living and be able to take care of myself if somebody else didn't come along and do it for me. It was the '70's, and my parents were worried about the fact that I traveled a lot, that I lived with people I wasn't related to, that I wasn't getting married and I didn't want to. I didn't shave my legs and I wore hiking boots and I didn't dress like a girl. It wasn't that I insisted on their understanding my work. I would argue with my mother about our political differences and about moral questions. In that sense it was more like two competing contemporaries in that I insisted that she hear my point of view and she insisted that I hear hers. But there was never a word of complaint from my father. He was just hoping I would make a living, and right up until I published my second book, he was saying I should come back home and work in the insurance office. My mother was much more vocal."

Phillips' political views were formed more by the Vietnam War than by any other event in her life. Few other political issues were so obvious. The de facto segregation so common in America didn't exist in Buckhannon. "There were only three or four black families and they were all related to one another. Their kids were actually very much accepted, but in a particular way. They had lots of friends, and some of the boys played sports. One of the black girls was a majorette, which was the premium social triumph for any girl. Yet, none of the white boys would have thought to ask her out on a date. It just wasn't allowed. At proms she would show up with a cousin or a black boy from a bigger town. I still communicate with some of those people. Some stayed in Buckhannon and some left. Of those who stayed, most of those who made successes were boys."

Phillips' independent streak became public when she was a senior in high school. The moratorium against the Vietnam War was held in Washington and protestors were asked to wear black armbands. "A group of us did, and the school was so alarmed that they called each one of us into the office and said we were going to be suspended unless we took the armbands off."

Some of her high school friends died in Vietnam, but both her brothers escaped the war. "I grew up being tortured by my older brother," she recalls, "not in a horrible way, but there was a lot of rivalry that suddenly changed when I was about 14 and his friends started liking me. Then he became more protective. I had a very close relationship with my younger brother because he was only 15 months younger than I was, and we grew up playing together. I feel very connected to both my brothers now, even though our lives have taken very different directions."

Phillips' relationship with her brothers was also reflected through the characters in *Machine Dreams*. She sees that novel as the story of a family bracketed by World War II and Vietnam and the fact that people in small isolated towns were used as cannon fodder. "I wrote that book as a warning that people often don't realize that they need to protect their families from their own governments, or they need to get involved with those governments, because if they don't, they will find their families threatened. The reason that so many people protested that war was that everybody was at risk. Now, with the volunteer army drawing basically from the underclass who sign up because they need financial support or a college education, it is an even more dangerous situation."

Phillips' identifies with all the characters in *Machine Dreams*—not only Jean, the mother, but also Billy and Mitch, the brothers. "I felt just as invested in the male characters as the women. I grew up being chastised for being too male—not that I was heavily involved in sports, but more that I thought that way or wrote that way. Once when I was in college, I sent some of my work to Robert Bly and he wrote back saying that I wrote like a man and that was a mistake. I sympathize strongly with those male characters because in that part of the country, in that kind of culture, the men have nowhere to go. They are taught from the very beginning that their lives are defined by the work that they do, yet they are living in a place in which work is unstable and hard to come by. "So much in them is unspoken and extremely complex and expressed only in subtle ways."

The women in these areas are imprisoned in a different way, Phillips believes, because they have vibrant emotional lives and tend to have intense articulate relations with one another. "I think in the past people didn't expect so much from the marriage relationship. It was more about family and providing for the family. I grew up in a place where people didn't have vast ambitions for themselves. It is amazing to me even now that so many people I went to high school with have settled right there in that area. They're managing their parents' businesses or reduced versions of their parents' businesses. I think of them as having a kind of unity or completion in their lives that I'll probably never have because I left. There is something to be said about being of a place all of your life because you are still living in a place that you feel intensely connected to. You know every corner of it. You know the people who live there back for several generations. You are concerned with your job, your work and your family. You have real roots. I think there must be a sense of achievement in moving from being one of the kids who grew up in the town to being one of the people running it.

"Psychologically I still feel a strong pull to that land. The reason I didn't finally settle in northern California, which is just beautiful, with the ocean and the incredible landscape, is because it felt, finally, so alien to me. I couldn't believe it was real. So I ended up coming back to the Northeast. Psychologically, somehow it works for me, because the land here is more like West Virginia. There are seasons and green trees and even dirt roads, if you get far enough back in the western part of the state."

Phillips agrees with the theory that until you leave a place you're not able to write about it as well as when you were living there. "In a sense you have no need to write about it if you are in it, if you are of it, although writers may leave because they are not of it. Yet there is something in them from the beginning that owes a complete fidelity to the place. But the observer always stands apart. You are no longer an instinctual animal, you are making distinctions and comparisons and connections. You attempt to redeem the place by heart.

"And when I say redeem, I don't mean that the place has gone wrong in any way. It has more to do with the place that has vanished. Families vanish. Everyone's family vanishes. We all leave whatever primary family we come from. And regardless of how screwed up that family was, or how "dysfunctional," it is such a part of our first sense of identity. In order to know what it was, artists are not recreating it, but creating different versions of it. More than transforming history, writers are saving that history from vanishing. The town that I lived in has vanished, but it exists in some form in my work. I suppose *Shelter* was an attempt at putting together a sense of what represented the underpinnings of those small towns, what the actual land was like, the primal force the place had."

In *Shelter* the setting does seem primal, and so thoroughly ingrained in the characters' lives and actions that there could be no other conceivable place for the action to occur. In fact, the setting appropriately supports Phillips' contention that her religious affiliation is pagan mysticism, although she was brought up as a Methodist. Her mother was a Sunday School teacher for 22 years, a Presbyterian who moved over to Methodism when she married. "My father, though," says Phillips, "hated organized religion. He went to church when his kids were christened, and that was it. This was another point where my parents differed. My mother went to church every Sunday and took the kids, and we sat through church service from the time we were seven. I soaked it up as atmosphere in a kind of osmosis; I wasn't that interested in what the minister was saying. My thoughts truly wandered. But as a world and a culture, with such sensual elements, it made an impression, and I'm glad that I experienced it.

"I don't remember paying any particular attention to a doctrine, even though I joined the church and at the time I took it very seriously. Later I knew it wasn't something I would continue to do on my own, and I haven't. To me, Eastern religion and Buddhism and Taoism are more representative of the way I sense the world working. I think religion is basically a reflection of culture, but I appreciate having been a part of the culture in that way."

Her parents' differences eventually led to divorce when Phillips was in high school. She describes her father as being "like most men from that part of the country—rather silent and inarticulate. His life was based on his work and what he did." It is not surprising that one of her themes is alienation within families. "I don't know a family in which alienation does not exist in one degree or another. The standard that we are being held up to is some kind of Waltons fantasy. It was a fantasy when the Waltons were a family. I think that difficulties in families have become much more apparent because women now have the option of leaving, and they certainly didn't have that option until nearly the mid-point of this century.

"My father was very strong in some ways. He had an incredible dignity and he was very meticulous. His clothes were always perfectly clean. I think he considered himself to be very much involved in the family. He didn't drink. He didn't leave. He was like most men in that time and place, and a man who wasn't like that would have been considered odd. In general, men weren't expected to have long discussions about anything. That's just the way it was. So in that sense, my family was not so different from many other families, except that my parents were estranged from each other pretty early on. My father had rigid ideas about women and other issues that stemmed from growing up with all the prejudices of the area.

"My mother had prejudices, too, but hers had been mitigated by her education, by being in the working world, and by dealing with people, and I think there wasn't enough in the relationship to hold them together. We had always lived in the house that my father had designed and built, but my mother moved the family into town when I was about 16. My father did not want to leave his house, but she insisted. She told him that if he didn't come, she would do it on her own. She had a job, she could get credit. So my father moved with us and then within three years my mother asked him to leave."

The house used as a setting in *Machine Dreams* was the house her father had built:

> She imagined her mother's room: the big antique bed, the L-shaped bank of windows, the Victorian bureau and its tall mirror bordered with knobs and spires. In Billy's room, just the other side of the shelves, there were twin beds on opposite walls. Usually Mitch slept in one of them and Danner heard her father's snoring behind the sound of the radio. His sleep was labored, oblivious. The sounds didn't seem like her father at all but became instead the rhythmic workings of the house, the blind labor that got them all through the night.

During her childhood in West Virginia, Phillips went off to many summer camps, usually for one or two weeks at a time. Although she has used fragmentary details from her own experiences in her novel, she created the camp in *Shelter* essentially to convey the theme that she was building rather than recreating a place that had actually existed all in one piece:

> Concede the heat of noon in summer camps. The quarters wavering in bottled heat, cots lined up in the big dark rooms that are pitch black if you walk in out of the sun. Black, quiet, empty, and the screen door banging shut three times behind you. Allowed in alone only if you are faint. Perhaps the heat has come over you, settled in from above and sucked your insides until you must lie down to sleep in the empty cabin while the rest are at hiking or canoes or archery. Now you lie there sleeping and the room is heavy and warm, but cooler than noon, the rough wooden walls exuding shade. . . . You are frightened because it is you

here with the future. And they are scattered along
Mud River walk, obscured by dense leaves, their
occasional cries no louder than the sounds of the
invisible birds.

It is difficult, Phillips maintains, to explain to people
that certain characters in her novels are not completely
real people, but represented only by pieces of them. For
example, the mother Jean in *Machine Dreams* represents
only aspects of Phillips' own mother. "Any time you
have a portrait of a character in a book," she says, "it's a
very limited picture. There is no way that a presentation
of a character in a book can equal or represent a real person. Place and time come across in a more complete way
in my fiction. The town of Buckhannon, the smells, the
heat, the sense of Main Street and the store fronts, is
very much a part of *Machine Dreams* and of some of the
stories in *Black Tickets.* My sense of the land itself is
very much the basis of the world in *Shelter.* That novel is
a more unadulterated take on the way time and place
seep into a book in a much more obvious way."

Living in one place for a long time, particularly during all the childhood years, she says, is always a great
advantage for a writer. "I think the reason that I experienced mobility and rootlessness was because I had
known the opposite, and I could make distinctions
about both states of being."

Her leaving—first in the summers beginning when
she was 18, and later, for good—is one of the most mysterious and alluring aspects of Jayne Anne Phillips' personal
history. Her stories of social and political alienation tend
to make readers picture her as daring and reactionary, so
her intrinsic compassion for the human spirit often sur-
prises those who expect a more cold-blooded take on life.

The transformation comes from the fact that, at the same time she shows us the unconventional side of life, she shows us how it works, and she does so without apology. In the story "Rayme," from *Fast Lanes,* she begins:

> In our student days we were all in need of fortune tellers. No one was sure what was happening in the outside world and no one thought about it much. We had no televisions and we bought few newspapers. Communal life seemed a continual dance in which everyone changed partners, a patient attempt at domesticity by children taking turns being parents. We were adrift but we were together. A group of us floated among several large ramshackle houses, houses arranged above and below each other on steep streets: a gritty version of terraced dwellings in some exotic Asia. The houses were old and comfortable, furnished with an accumulation of overstuffed chairs and velveteen sofas gleaned from rummage sales. . . . Houses of the student ghetto were the landscape of the dream—a landscape often already condemned.

The first summer she traveled—at the end of her freshman year at West Virginia University in Morgantown—Phillips worked in an amusement park in Ohio. The next year she worked on the Cape and after that she traveled back and forth across the country. From the experience of that travel, and from living in houses with people she "wasn't related to," Phillips gained an empathy for those who had stepped over the edge of conventional American life. "Anybody living in this country should be aware that not everyone has a home to go back to or even wants one," she says. "I don't find it odd or unusual to represent a cross-section of lives in my stories. These characters aren't based on specific people— they're composites of people I have met or imagined. The transformation happens when the writer imagines being this or that person. I suppose I wasn't limited to being a good girl, living in one particular way and staying on one particular track."

Jayne Anne Phillips is continually involved in a spiritual process. "There is something about writing that is almost religious in nature. I think we write to find out what things mean and how one thing is connected to another. What it comes down to is whether anything means anything. The whole process of writing is basically a statement of faith that life is not just random, and as writers we both observe it and understand and create it. Art within a culture or a society operates both as a kind of probing, investigatory celebration and a sort of conscience.

"A novel becomes the center of my psychic life for several years, and it becomes a movement through various dimensions that I don't really direct consciously. In that sense it can't be mistaken, just as we can't say, 'That dream was wrong.' There is a truism in the very being of a book. It is as if you understand it by living it at every level of yourself." Presently, Phillips is immersed in writing a novel tentatively titled *Mother Care*.

Even though her explanation of the novel writing process has a slightly Buddhist slant, she says she can't completely accept the idea of reincarnation. "That's a religious story in the same way the virgin birth is a religious story, but it is true in the spiritual sense that we live many times within our own lives, if we live right, and certainly the writer or the artist lives many lives. That's in a sense the greatest privilege about the process of writing. "

Jayne Anne Phillips has been almost everywhere, but she is still thinking about how far she might yet go. "That whole Buddhist thing about reaching cosmic consciousness and not coming back?" she says. "I have to admit, I'm not so interested in reaching cosmic consciousness. I want to come back forever."

Excerpt from *Shelter:*

Concede the heat of noon in summer camps. the quarters wavering in bottled heat, cots lined up in the big dark rooms that are pitch black if you walk in out of the sun. Black, quiet, empty, and the screen door banging shut three times behind you. Allowed in alone only if you are faint. Perhaps the heat has come over you, settled in from above and sucked your insides until you must lie down to sleep in the empty cabin while the rest are at hiking or canoes or archery. Now you lie there sleeping and the room is heavy and warm, but cooler than noon, the rough wooden walls exuding shade. The cots are precisely mute. Identical and different in olive-green blankets, each pulled tight and tucked. In your mind, you see the bodies lying there, each in its own future. You are frightened because it is you here with the future. And they are scattered along Mud River walk, obscured by dense leaves, their occasional cries no louder than the sounds of the invisible birds. Or they are standing in line before bright targets stretched across baled hay. They are holding taut bows straight out, pulling back on the strings with all their strength.

School photo courtesy of John Marius.

RICHARD MARIUS

"The past is a story and we know the past finally by the stories we tell about it."

Picture a small farm in Dixie Lee Junction, near Lenoir City, Tennessee, in the early 1940's. The muted sound of traffic on Highway 70 to the north of the property and Highway 11 to the east can be heard through the stout walls of the house, reminding the family that lives there of the expanding suburban encroachment. To the south, Old Stage Road borders the land, and on the west it is insulated by woods. Inside the house, it is quiet except for the staccato click of a typewriter. A small boy is seated at a table, picking out keys on the old manual machine his mother had used years before as a reporter. The child is Richard Marius, and this is the beginning of his apprenticeship as a writer.

Now a professor at Harvard University, Marius attributes most of his success as a fiction writer to three factors: "a love for the English language, the experiences of a vividly remembered childhood, and my profession as a historian."

In appearance, Marius, with his thick, graying mustache and his penchant for old-fashioned bow ties, looks very much the academician. Tall, handsome, and physically fit, he rarely drives anywhere he can ride a bicycle or walk. He has bicycled across France several times and when he taught at The University of Tennessee in Knoxville, he sometimes walked home from campus—a distance of seven miles. At Harvard he walks the same distance back and forth to his house in Belmont, and in warm weather he rides his bicycle. Marius has pursued his academic career and his avocation as a fiction writer in the same way—with an unflagging energy. But getting there came by way of a circuitous route.

The second son and third child of Henri Marius, a Greek immigrant and foundryman, and his wife Eunice, Richard Marius learned to read and write early. His mother helped him decipher the comic pages when he was four years old. "I don't ever remember a time when I didn't want to write," Marius claims. And you have to believe him, because he seems to recall everything else about his childhood. His early impressions—the farm, the house his father built by hand, the events of his own life as well as those of his parents, both told and experienced firsthand—have found their way into his three novels, and another book is soon to be completed.

When he talks about the past, Marius seems almost to be transported there, to that beloved farm where he grew up, to those open, grassy fields and the deep, shady woods, to the close-knit rural community and the small Baptist church that was the focal point of neighborhood and family life. His is the typical nostalgic memory of endless summer days when anything is possible. His voice, tinged with pleasure, has a way of sliding down an "ohhh" that exudes unqualified delight in his boyhood. "I remember the sun rising to the east and throwing its light into my upstairs room that I inherited from my older sister Nancy when she left home, and I recall with special delight the way the trees in the woods broke up the setting sun so that shafts of light and shadow streamed through space, giving the world a magical look. When I was a child the farm seemed enormous, although in fact it was only about 20 acres, and then later my father bought five acres at $200 an acre from John Ginn, an old farmer in the neighborhood who had ruined the soil by planting corn in it year after year."

Through the character of Paul Alexander, who is patterned after his father Henri, Marius describes the farm in the beginning of *After the War* (Alfred A. Knopf, 1992): "Tonight I sit at my kitchen table and look over the darkened hillside pasture towards my lower field, where lespedeza hay grows lush in the summer dark. I can smell the heat—a baked, hard smell. . . . Beyond the lower field in our shallow valley runs the two-lane highway to Nashville. The lights of passing cars blaze at intervals. Sometimes a truck rumbles by, and the sound carries up to me at this mysterious hour when a rural world is fast asleep."

His early years were spent roaming the farm and nearby fields, and spending time where his father worked in Lenoir City—the car works, a railroad establishment that manufactured box cars for Southern Railway. "I grew up around trains," he says fondly, "crawling in and out of them, climbing up into locomotives, sitting while railroad men talked. When my father went there in 1917, boxcars were still made of wood. At a certain point—I believe it was 1931—the Interstate Commerce Commission ruled that boxcars had to be made of metal. When a train derailed, boxcars turned to matchsticks if they were made of wood. Once upon a time every freight car on Southern Railway rolled on wheels manufactured under my father's supervision at Lenoir City. When I was in New Orleans during the horrible year I spent in seminary down there, I used to see the trains go by, knowing that every car with 'Southern Serves the South' on the side rolled on wheels made by my father."

By the time he was six, Marius would regularly walk a mile by himself to the Munsey farm where Sam Munsey and his "big tribe" of boys worked to wrestle a living from the small acreage or "I sat with Mrs. Ginn on her spacious front porch," Marius recalls, "and helped her churn butter. When the war came, things changed. The boys went off to service, the neighborhood seemed to empty."

The war in fact changed the whole character of the countryside. The construction of Fort Loudon Dam by the Tennessee Valley Authority brought in hundreds of workers, many of whom lived in a trailer park adjoining the highway junction nearby. "For the first time," Marius remembers, "I had lots of playmates my own age. Tough kids, I might add." And when Oak Ridge was built beginning about 1943, the tranquility of the countryside disappeared. Farragut, where Marius was in grammar school, overflowed with newcomers. Students were crowded in, and discipline was difficult to maintain. "At a certain moment," Marius says, "I became terribly bored with the farm, but the result was that I became an avid reader. Mother was more or less drafted to work at Oak Ridge during the war, and I remember long, boring days. In 1945 she quit her job just before the atom bomb was dropped and she took my brother

John and me to Philadelphia. I had never been so excited in my life, and I wanted from then on to be a city person. Yet I still remember with such fondness the intensity of sensations on the farm—the light, the power of storms (I've always been afraid of lightning), the parade of the seasons, the moods of nature. I loved all that, and it stays with me when I write."

There was always the impulse to tell and listen to stories. In *After the War,* Marius' character Brian Ledbetter says that if a man cannot tell stories, he has not lived. And in relating to Paul Alexander his own experiences during the Civil War, Ledbetter reflects the sentiment of all storytellers: "He looked happily around in his aged brightness, unable for a moment to believe in the good fortune of having someone hear his story for the first time. He fastened his sharp eyes on me and cleared his throat and spoke carefully, like a man just remembering something not thought of in a long while, as if he had just decided to tell a tale never framed in words before, carving it all anew and taking care to get it exactly right, for if he did not get it exactly right, something would die. It was all there, in lines honed and polished and stacked in clean rows in his mind so that to move one was to set them all in motion."

Marius' own storytelling talents emerged early. His sharp perceptions of the world around him gave him a keen observation. "When I was in the fifth grade," he says, "I actually typed out a newspaper for my school on my mother's typewriter. I typed out five or six copies at a time—I didn't have access to a mimeograph machine—and I passed around those copies at school. After I did that a few times, though, I contracted whooping cough and had to be out of school for about two months, and that ended the paper. It was my year of childhood sickness."

Marius' desire to write was fueled by incessant reading—Zane Gray, Mark Twain, Poe. "We had a copy of Poe's complete works and I read that absolutely all the way through. And I read Kipling. My mother and father had lived in Burma for a while, and Mother came home with a great love of Kipling. We had a big volume of his short stories which I read again and again and again. In fact, I still think one of the greatest stories in the English language is "The Man Who Would Be King." It is, I think, even better than *Heart of Darkness*.

"I read all of Sherlock Holmes, anything and everything I could find. In fact, at Farragut School we had two bus pick-ups—first and second load. I was on second load, so I had to stay after school every day for about an hour and fifteen minutes to wait for the bus. I sat in the library and read. On bright days I might roam around outside, but sometimes even in bright weather I sat and read until I had read just about everything in the school library."

Marius remembers an episode in the seventh grade when he discovered that someone had left a senior English literature book on the steps where the buses loaded. After it had sat there for several days, Marius began to look forward to picking up the book and reading from it until his bus arrived. Every day the book would be there and every day he read further in it and every day he put it back on the steps for the mysterious owner, but it stayed on the steps long enough for him to finish the entire book. "I was just so hungry to read things," he said. "I can even remember the cover. It was green with a white floral design." Books also play an important role in the lives of his fictional characters. In *After the War,* Paul, Darcy Coolidge, the Colonel and Daisy are all avid readers.

Richard Marius' life as a child had been preordained eight years before his birth, when his older brother Jim was born with Down Syndrome. Eunice Marius was terrified when she discovered herself pregnant with a third child, because her doctor had instructed her not to have any more children. A deeply religious Southern Baptist, Mrs. Marius prayed constantly that God would let her baby be born healthy. In return, she promised she would do all she could to see that the child would be a servant for God. So when Richard Marius was born in 1933, he was told from the beginning of his life that he was a special child destined to serve God. "All those years," Marius says, "I remember my mother taking me aside and saying, very quietly, 'I know God has a great work for you to do because I prayed so hard that you would be normal.'

"It was just something I naturally assumed, so when I decided to become a minister my senior year in high school, it seemed the only thing to do. I remember thinking, 'This is why I was born.'"

Except that, as it turned out, a series of events interrupted his religious education, and Marius ended up being a teacher and a writer. Although that was a grievous disappointment to his mother, it wasn't much of a surprise to those who had followed his literary progress. Even as a boy he had an eye for concrete detail and a reporter's talent for observation. Images of his childhood—places, people, colors, names, quotes, even smells and sounds—remain as vivid in his mind today as when he first observed them. He can remember titles of childhood books he read, quotes from writers who have impressed him, conversations with his parents or teachers or friends. He transfers to paper almost verbatim those scenes that are still preserved in his head. He is a great talker, too, and he can quote snatches of conversation from the distant past as if they had been spoken yesterday. Even events that occurred before he was born sound immediate in his telling of them. For example, his recall of his parents' three-year stay in Burma makes the story sound as if he had been a first-hand observer rather than a child who would not be born for 13 years:

> My parents went to Burma when Dad got a job with a British corporation called Burma Mines. Herbert Hoover had discovered a silver mine from the Ming Dynasty up near the Chinese border, and the British decided to exploit it because the 'natives' liked hard silver money better than paper money. Dad married Mother on December 2, 1918, and they left immediately for Burma. The first thing Dad did was to work as an engineer, building a power line across the Northern Shan States from central Burma. The smelter was located at a town called Nam Thu above Lashio, which became a terminus for the Burma Road during World War II. My sister Nancy was born in a British Army hospital in a town called Maimio, and the nurse who cared for Mother had cared for Dad when he was in the hospital in London. After about three years Mother got terribly homesick, and so they returned to the United States. I have some letters Mother wrote home . . . and I always thought that their time in Burma was the happiest period of their lives.

In fact the past is integral in his writing and his life, and a few years ago when he found in his parents' old farmhouse the journal he had kept daily in the years

1948 and 1949, it was a precious discovery. "I was struck," he recalls with excitement, "that almost every entry begins with the sentence, 'Today has been a wonderful day!' And we did have wonderful times. We were out in the country, riding horses and playing games and camping, and though because of our religion we were not allowed to dance, we acted in plays and played football and baseball and basketball. We were going to church all the time, but some of those times we were having parties or picnics at church, or singing." Although he accepted the condition of his brother Jim as the way things were, as part of God's plan, Marius and the other children in the family—his older sister Nancy and his younger brother John—sometimes felt emotionally slighted by their parents' attention to their brother. For a brief period when Marius was a child, Jim was sent to a special school in New Jersey, but his parents grieved so much at his absence that they brought him back home. "I think we always felt that Mother and Dad had no ability to discipline Jim or deny him, and I think Dad's affection for him was much greater than it was for any of us," Marius says. "I came to recognize all that as natural, but at times it was hard. Jim used to play the radio and the phonograph so loud that I could hardly think, and it was difficult to study at home except late at night. Dad would always say, 'It's the only pleasure he has.' I think it made me a night owl. But I certainly did not walk around feeling resentment or bitterness about the whole thing. And I don't feel any such bitterness now. That was the way things were."

Accepting "the way things were" was common in those days. "Some people in the community were very poor," says Marius, "and some were reasonably well off, but we all liked each other and were happy in each other's company. There wasn't anybody who was exiled or ostracized in any way."

That is, except for the black community. Like many children of the post-Civil War South, Marius at first took for granted the social position of blacks in the area, but as he grew older he began to see southern racial laws as horrendous, particularly those in his own home town. Although blacks and whites worked side by side all day at the car works in Lenoir City, at the 3:30 whistle, the black workers left and walked down the railroad tracks to the little settlement where they lived below Lenoir City and where they were required by law to be off the streets after six o'clock at night.

For the first years, black people seemed to be only on the periphery of his life except for a black hand who worked at the house and a nearby black neighbor who raised cotton. "Our hand's name was Anderson," says Marius. "I remember once when he was sitting at our kitchen table and drinking coffee—I was about three years old—I was playing under the table and I noticed the electric cord of the percolator hanging down. I pulled the cord and the coffee pot came down on top of me and scalded my arm. I still remember Anderson grabbing me up and comforting me that day. It is one of my earliest memories.

"I remember, too, Uncle Ben Bacchus, a Negro farmer who lived down near the river. He had been born in Alabama and he still managed to raise cotton in East Tennessee. I used to walk down and talk to him a lot. I even wrote a story about him later when I worked on the *Lenoir City News*. After he died I walked down to see his wife and we were commiserating about our mutual sadness when she told me that he came to see her every night. 'He comes as a little dot of light,' she told me, 'and the light dances around the room when I talk to him.' I've never forgotten that story," says Marius, "or how touched I was by it."

But those encounters were personal, limited. It was not until 1949, on a train ride through Alabama en route to a University of Tennessee football game with his father that Marius realized the social and economic plight of blacks in the South. "I was amazed at the numbers of black people I saw. It was October and there were thousands in the fields picking cotton." Marius' growing sense of social injustice became evident in his political activism a few years later at a Billy Graham rally at The University of Tennessee where then-President Nixon appeared. Marius joined protestors of the Vietnam War in disrupting the president's speech, and his participation was met with disdain in Lenoir City, where he had always been regarded with pride. "Oh, Mrs. Marius," a friend said to his mother at church, "I am so sorry for you."

"I think we were the last generation of writers to experience a South that was truly slow and rural and very poor," Marius says. "The hangover from the Depression was absolutely crucial to understanding people like me. I was born in 1933, and that shaped everything in my life." His fascination with the past has been a critical factor in his work. In an interview in *Contemporary Authors* he says that 'any historian is perhaps nothing more than a weaver of glittering illusion, as fragile as light and as dangerous as poison.' Marius laughs now when he is read his own statement. "That sounds very grandiloquent," he says, chuckling, "but what I mean by that is that the past is a story and we know the past finally by the stories we tell about it. We have statistics about the past and we have raw data about the past. We even have archeology, but we don't really understand the past until we tell a story about it and that story is sometimes told so well that we imagine it is true; but in fact a well told story about the past can be simply an illusion, and yet we live on those kinds of illusions. In my first novel, *The Coming of Rain,* my whole point was to imagine a woman who convinced her son absolutely that the past was one way when in fact it was radically different from the way she presented it. The power of her story was a way of making an illusion that was very convincing, at least to her son, but in the end it was not true." That woman, Sarah Beckwith, was modeled after Marius' mother Eunice. Early in the novel she says to her son Sam, "It was the answer to the prayer I made to the Lord—that I'd have a son. And I did! God gave you to me, Sam. You were not an ordinary child. You were a gift of God."

That was one kind of illusion, but Marius says that when he talks about the "Confederate myth of the lost cause," he is talking about illusion, too. He refers to the Civil War as the "Gone with the Wind" fraud. "I think that movie was probably the most important aesthetic experience of the arts that my generation of southerners had. By the time I was in high school I had seen it eight times, and then when I saw it in college for the ninth time I realized what an extraordinarily painfully racist film it was. It also gives you an entirely mythological view of the South. In every way that one piece of writing can be a rebellion against another piece of writing, *The Coming of Rain* was a rebellion against *Gone with the*

Wind. Marius hesitates and laughs. "My novel was not as successful with the public as *Gone with the Wind,* I might add. Certainly there has been no national debate over who should play the role of Sarah Beckwith."

What about the long-contended theory that Southern writing is different from "other" writing? Marius supports the claim, saying that southerners use literature to transform history. "Hemingway didn't write about the past," he reflects. "John Updike doesn't write about the past. But the southern writer nearly always writes about the past, especially the kind of southern writer who is now dying off. He or she is confronted with the past and with writing about families and with coming to terms with the differences between the writer and the world around him. You simply cannot imagine writers like Proust or Marquand or Wharton or Updike coming out of the South. Their writing is usually about people in intellectual circles where the conversation and allusions are highly cerebral. *Mosquitoes,* Faulkner's attempt to write an intellectual southern novel, was a terrible failure. Southerners are much more likely to write about violence and religion and the family, and, of course—the past—than are writers elsewhere."

Marius points out that while the southern writer is decidedly a part of his own society, he is often also alienated from it at the same time. "The great line of southern writing," he says, is Quentin's quote at the end of Faulkner's *Absalom, Absalom,* when Shreve says to Quentin, "'Now I want you to tell me just one thing more. Why do you hate the South?'

"And Quentin says, 'I don't hate it, I don't hate it. . . . I don't. I don't! I don't hate it! I don't hate it!'"

In a piece in the *Sewanee Review,* Marius wrote: "I bristle when anyone calls me a 'southern' writer. I am a novelist of the border, and in both my novels, the romantic traditions of the old South take a good beating. I shall beat those traditions still more in my third."

Ironically, Marius himself seems almost to have grown up in his own southern novel. His life has all the elements of plot, setting, and characters vital to the southern Gothic story. For example, alienation: Until he made peace with his sister Nancy just before her early death from lung cancer, the two had been estranged for years, and Nancy herself had been jealously guarded by an overprotective father with Greek traditions and old-world philosophies about women. Religion: The religious theme so indispensable to a southern novel comes out in his mother's promise to God, using the young Richard as ransom. Guilt: There is guilt both on the part of his mother for having an imperfect child, and later, on the part of his father for not having interfered with his wife's plan for Richard. The imperfect child: The damaged brother or sister is often an essential factor in the southern novel, almost as vital as the all-important connection to the land and family and the acute sense of history. And wasn't Marius the wayward son, departing from the path chosen for him by his mother? Finally, there is his inevitable breakdown with the disintegration of his religious beliefs, following immediately on the heels of the realization that the world was much bigger than the 20-acre perimeters of the farm at Dixie Lee Junction. The single element that is out of place in the classic southern novel is the happy connection between Marius and his younger brother John, with whom he still shares a loving relationship.

Almost any writer who grew up in the South in the first half of this century has been strongly affected by the ravages of the Civil War upon family and community. On the Bradley County farm where she was born in 1891, Marius' mother grew up with a plethora of Civil War stories. Her family was both Quaker and Federal, so all of the men except for one young boy who was her uncle left the farm and went north to avoid the Confederate draft." My great-grandfather," says Marius, "was also a Quaker who worked in a salt mine for the Federal Army. His son George was a teamster for the Federals and he drove horses and mules under fire. The Methodist side of the family, of course, could fight for the cause, and my great-grandmother's sister married a man named Flagg, and their son, Henry Lee Flagg, organized the first Tennessee Cavalry of the Federal Army.

"My aunt Doll Lawson died in her 80's when I was 12 years old. She was born during the Civil War and she had an absolutely contemptuous hatred of the Confederates, because the Confederates in Bradley County, knowing my family were Federals, were very hard on them." In two of his novels, Marius uses the character Brian Ledbetter to give voice to southerners' participation in the Federal Army during the Civil War. When Marius was still enamored of *Gone with the Wind,* he felt sorry that his ancestors had been in the Federal Army instead of the Confederate Army because it seemed so much more romantic. "Now, of course," he says, "I am hugely proud of them."

Marius the writer takes the past back even another generation, when in *After the War* he creates the character of Bernal and Guy, ghosts of Paul's comrades during the First World War. "For one thing," Marius says, "they're stolen out of Henry James, *The Turn of the Screw*. The characters are a means of accentuating the encounter between the past and present and Paul's coming to a new country and having to adapt to another life. I thought, 'If they were real ghosts, they would be jealous that Paul was gradually forgetting them. So that's how I made them. It was really more of an aesthetic than a device. I was touched in reading a book about Vietnam vets by a psychiatrist here in Cambridge. He said that very often the veterans would continue to talk to their buddies who were killed in Vietnam. And my father told me about feeling guilty because his friends were killed in 1914 and he survived. He said they were still very vivid in his memory, so I came up with the idea of using Bernal and Guy. It was also a means of using a flashback in a different way."

Although he has left the South in body, Marius still lives there in spirit. Since 1978 he has taught at Harvard University and lived in Cambridge, Massachusetts, with his second wife Lanier Smythe, an artist. Yet, two of his three southern novels have been written in Cambridge, and he has just completed a fourth, a sequel to *After the War* that is to be called *An Affair of Honor.* Marius agrees with Elizabeth Spencer that a southerner always remains a southerner, no matter where he or she travels. "You write about your place," he says, "and it is exotic to you, and you write about it because you come in contact with another place and it drives you back to your place in a way that is very different from the other places you've been. Faulkner went off to Europe in 1925 and came home and published *Soldier's Pay,* and Hemingway went off to Europe and started writing about Spain and Italy. The southern writer always comes back and writes about the South." With tongue in cheek he adds, "It's wonderful to be a southern literary person in Boston. People think you are so exotic."

Because of the insulation of southern towns, childhood heroes tended to be scaled-down versions of more herculean models. Out in the country, Marius says, you didn't see heroes, but you had inspiring teachers, and Richard Marius' childhood heroes were his first grade teacher, Miss Elsie Lewellyn, and his seventh grade teacher, Miss Hattie Simmons Witt. Why? Because they both read to their classes at the end of every school day. "Miss Witt read one story that impressed me that I was later to read in French—*Sans Famille*—about how a boy named Ramie travels across the country with a man named Francois. Miss Witt had pronounced it Fran-co-is, but I didn't mind discovering that. It was an enthralling story and she was such a wonderful influence on my reading and writing. I shall never forget her."

Reading, writing, and listening became Richard Marius' preoccupations as a child. And listening to his mother read the Bible endowed him with a sense of rhythm that he still uses as a benchmark for his own work. That harmonious sense of syntax is essential to good writing, and though it is difficult to define, the true writer knows it when he hears it. The biblical rhythms of King James still run through his head when Marius is revising and refining text but aside from admiring the poetry and lyrics of the Bible, Marius can no longer view the church with the unquestioning faith he had as a child. "My mother's philosophy was the dominant force in my early life—that the Bible was literally true and that God watched over us at every moment and if we didn't believe in God as the Almighty Savior, we would go to hell.

Mother believed very much in prophecy and talked end-lessly about the end of the world. It was her whole con-versation. Somehow I realized early in life that Mother was very much afraid of death and that in some sense her intense effort to talk continually about the certainty of prophecy—that Jesus would come again—was the hope that kept her from the fear of death."

When Marius pursued the vocation "he was born for," and started his freshman year at The University of Tennessee, a single intellectual episode changed the entire direction of his life. In a freshman English course he read a book called *Ideas for Writing,* which con-tained an essay by Princeton philosopher W. T. Stace. Stace argued against what Aristotle called "final cause"—that everything exists for a reason and that God has planned all the world. "It was as though I had been standing inside an enormous brick building," says Marius, "and it all suddenly crumbled to powder around me. The realization that everything that Stace said must be true and everything that my mother had told me must be false plunged me into a terrific depression. It was the summer of 1951, I was 17 years old, and back then you didn't go to a therapist, you just toughed it out. But I realize now that I had all the symptoms of a major clini-cal depression, it hit me so hard. That moment—that scene—is so vivid in my memory. I remember the class-room in Ayres Hall, and I remember a boy across the aisle—his white shirt—and it was a sunny day and I could see down the hill to downtown Knoxville. There was the Church Street Methodist Church, which was an imitation of a Gothic church that I realized was imitat-ing the faith of the Middle Ages and I remember think-ing, "'It's all illusion. None of it is true. All of this solidity of church buildings is an illusion to create out of stone the idea of a god who doesn't exist."

Still, he struggled with the idea that his entire life up until that moment had led him toward the seminary. Perhaps, he thought, he could make an adjustment to this new information and reshape his ministry and still continue along the path his mother had carved for him. So he went on to seminary in New Orleans, choosing it deliberately because it was fundamentalist. After a year, however, he was overwhelmed by depression, and he made plans to transfer to the Louisville Seminary. Then another twist of fate occurred when he was awarded a scholarship to go to France. "I spent the whole year in Paris reading people like Jean Paul Sartre and Camus, so by the time I came back I realized that I wanted to be an academician. I thought I could teach church history, which is what I studied at Yale, and it turned out to be great preparation for the Western Civilization course I taught at The University of Tennessee."

Roland H. Bainton, Marius' former teacher at Yale, claimed that he heard in Marius' later book on Luther "the reverberations of an agonized cry of frustration because the contemporary church has let the author down." Marius denies that his portrayal is personal. Rather, he says, his Luther evolved out of his "opposition to the Vietnam War and his efforts . . . to teach the Reformation." His goal was to present Luther as a real flesh and blood human being rather than an infallible cardboard hero.

As a Renaissance scholar, Marius' characterizations of historical figures are guided by the same precepts that he uses for characters in his novels. In a *National Forum* article, he said, "Writers observe in a world of restless change. In setting their observations on paper, all writers create something—a design that makes the observations make sense, something that relates them to the rest of our thought and feeling, something that may make them memorable."

Just as his mother used religion to ward off the fear of death, Marius uses his writing to make himself remembered. He has said that when he dies, his writing will be his legacy to the future, the thing that keeps him from perishing completely from this earth. But there is an old belief in the South that says as long as your name is written down somewhere, you will never be forgotten. Richard Marius' name appears now in novels, historical biographies, edited collections, and numerous other nonfiction books. Perhaps that is now, and will always be, a writer's best effort at thwarting oblivion.

Excerpt from *Bound for the Promised Land*

They moved up the valley of the North Platte now, very slowly, trundling their ten hours a day. Another wheel broke on Jason's wagon. Just splintered and fell apart, and they replaced it with the spare Adam and Samuel had brought across the river way back in Missouri.

The river lay on their right, running swiftly over its shallow, sandy bed. The trail came close to it, veered away, swung near again. And one day in the dead stillness of a hot, dusty afternoon, Adam looked ahead of them and saw blocks heaped up low against the horizon as though a child had left a playhouse there, a blue, curious spectacle. He showed them to the old man. The old man shaded his eyes, squinted and nodded and spat in the earth. "It's the Courthouse," he said. "They call that there Courthouse Rock."

The vision was uncanny. It rose slowly, imperially, gigantically, and as they crawled heavily toward it, the rock became a great, hulking fortress of stone asserting itself in celestial calm against the enormous sky, claiming dominion over the vast and level plain. As they came on and on, its very bulk, its peerless eminence, commanded their silent concentration. Adam looked at the Courthouse Rock and fell to musing. Their slow pace and the great rock drinking the sun and rising out of the flat plain captivated his sight and hypnotized him.

Jason, too, brooded at Courthouse Rock. He plunged along by his lead oxen, all alone in a world where he had found refuge from the deceit and injury of his companions in Ash Hollow. He did not even talk to Harry anymore. His eyes were fixed on the great shimmering rock, and he hardly looked where his feet were stepping.

The rock came nearer and grew bigger. There was an odd and terrifying threat in its almost imperceptibly swelling grandeur. They saw it all one night and all the next day, and on the second night it was large enough to block out the stars behind it. On the next morning it was there, emerging from the soft iridescence of dawn as they silently broke camp and moved on, the rock slowly taking the brightening sunshine and the rising heat like something huge, feeding on light and warmth and still growing. On the next night it was grander still, still ahead of them, off to the south and west, and Jason watched it with fixed, silent fascination, as if he were waiting for the rock to move or do something, and he did not dare take his eyes off it lest it quiver while he was looking away.

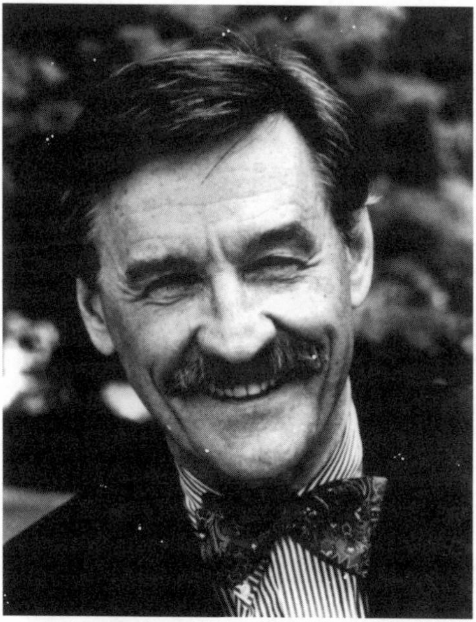

Photo courtesy of Alfred A. Knopf. © Nancy Crampton.

Photo courtesy of Elizabeth Cox.

ELIZABETH COX

"In the South there are a lot of secrets, some of them unconscious. The lack of tolerance and openness creates tension, which makes the place ripe for storytelling."

Shortly after the publication of Elizabeth Cox's first novel, *Familiar Ground,* she and her brother were sitting at lunch one day when her brother noticed that both her hands were balled into tight fists. He reached over to loosen the fingers, then changed his mind and shaped them back into fists. "You probably got a long way with your hands like that," he said.

Cox had indeed come a long way. "If you grow up female on the campus of an all-male school, you can get lost in a world of masculine expectation," says Cox. "My mother once suggested that I write a book entitled *I Was Raised in a Boy's Dormitory;* but I told her the title might prove to be the most interesting part."

When Cox, known as "Betsy," talks about her privileged childhood, her eyes glitter and her cheeks color with excitement. Blonde and blue-eyed, she gestures emphatically to punctuate various points as she reminisces about her years on the campus of Baylor School in Chattanooga, where her father, Herbert (Hub)

Bernard Barks, was headmaster. Although the school is now co-ed, Cox, born in 1942, grew up as the solitary girl among hundreds of male students, dozens of faculty, and two brothers.

"To my friends, my situation looked idyllic, but it wasn't. I did enjoy the male attention, but I wasn't fooled into believing that it told me anything about myself. I had to pull back into solitude and look closely at who I was and what I wanted. I became fiercely stubborn and grew heavily dependent upon place."

No child could have lived in a more picturesque setting. From the window of her childhood bedroom in Chattanooga, Tennessee, Elizabeth Cox could look out across the Tennessee River, beyond Williams Island, and into the gliding series of mountains that form the eastern range of the Appalachians. The view so inspired her that eventually it became a metaphor for her life—the winding, constantly changing river, the solitary island, and the enduring, immovable mountains. Later she transformed those visual images into what she calls "visceral" realizations that have affected not only her writing, but her personal life as well. "I think," says Cox, in her languid and pacifying southern accent, "because southerners love place so much, that what they say, what they write about, comes out of loving that place. The river taught me how to move, the island taught me how to be alone, and the mountains taught me how to remain.

"I watched the mountains—Signal Mountain, Elder Mountain, and Lookout Mountain—every day, and most nights. Growing up with that scene had a profound effect on me. The school campus covered more than 100 acres. I roamed that land in all seasons, either alone or with my brothers. We found Indian mounds, arrowheads, and every now and then something that looked like an ancient tool. We saw barges carrying coal and lumber. We saw bootleggers, chased by police, racing on motorboats to the island at night. In summer, rain moved down the river in long sheets and we tried to outrun it.

"I received a lot of attention, perhaps too much, just for being a girl," Cox says, "and though I enjoyed the fuss, I didn't feel really seen. I felt invisible, like something plastic, a doll. The only time I felt real was when I was alone. When I closed myself in my room, my mother thought I was sad; but I needed time alone. Growing up in such a social setting, I learned to be an extrovert, but my real strength is in being contemplative and interior."

In those contemplative periods, Cox was storing up the atmosphere that would later emerge in her stories, novels and poetry. In *Familiar Ground,* she transfers those intuitive realizations to her character Jacob, who as a young boy, experiences the same feelings that Cox had as a child. Also like Cox, he *felt* more than understood them:

> When Jacob rode on those trips, he would turn his head to watch the trees and fields that went by. Sometimes when he looked, as he turned his head, there was a moment, but only one moment, when he saw something he recognized, a space in the trees that hung above the ground; and he saw both the space and the ground, and the light on it. It was a clearing he thought he had seen before, even played in. . . .
>
> And Jacob understood why there are times when you pass some trees or a piece of land that takes your eye, that that land even seems to call, make you hear something; but upon closer inspection it falls from

you so that you feel a loss. Then you lean toward it as if you might find what you have missed, knowing it is important. But still, you feel a loss, because the whole seeing and hearing was within you and momentary, and there was no way to prolong the pleasure of it.

Except for her years away at college, Cox spent her first 21 years in Chattanooga and the shelter of living in two families: the smaller, tightly integrated family of her parents and brothers, and the larger, more elastic world of The Baylor School.

For the Barks family, learning was a way of life. Cox's mother was a vibrant and beautiful woman from Georgia whose friends called her "Duchess." Her humor permeated the entire campus. She also served as a mother figure to the dormitory boys away from home.

Cox's brothers, Herb and Coleman, were similarly affected by the influences of their upbringing. Herb Barks became a minister and followed in his father's footsteps as Baylor headmaster. He now serves as headmaster of The Hammond School in Columbia, South Carolina, and Coleman Barks is a poet who teaches at the University of Georgia.

Although Cox was writing poetry early in her childhood, it was nothing she was willing to show off. For the most part, she kept her poems secret in a small black book. "I grew up in an atmosphere where people talked about books all the time: the teachers were always talking about books, my parents were always reading, my brothers were always reading. We didn't read in order to talk about what we were reading, though. We read books in order to learn how to live our lives. The storytelling was like that, too.

"Every Friday night, my mother would serve refreshments to the Baylor boys who had to stay in study hall. They were the ones who had misbehaved or hadn't made their grades. She would give them refreshments and ask them to come over at 9 o'clock when they got out of study hall. Some of the teachers would come over, too, because Mother always had very good things to eat. I remember once, sitting in the recreation room with ping pong tables and everyone talking, that the Latin teacher, Mr. Pennington, was exclaiming passionately about something called the *Iliad.* I was probably about four, so what I absorbed more than the details of the story was the importance of it, the language and a way of talking about it that showed me that these teachers really loved teaching and were passionate about their subjects. That was the kind of atmosphere I grew up in. Nobody ever said, 'Oh, this is a good poem, write more of these. It was taken for granted that this was a part of our life.'

To give her a broader social experience, Cox's parents enrolled her in a Chattanooga public school outside the prep school gates. There, she discovered that her teachers liked what she was writing. "I was never good at writing academic papers, though," says Cox, laughing. "When I had to write research papers in college, I was always tempted to make up too many details. I wrote it the way I thought it should be. Writers make history more interesting."

It was her mother who had the most profound influence on her career as a writer, Cox says, more than she ever knew. "Both my parents brought something very different to my life. My father was devout, quiet and serious, but when he did talk, everyone listened because whatever he said was something you wanted to hear.

"Both my parents attended church regularly and took us with them—though I never felt religion was forced on me. My mother taught Bible in the school, and she often read it to me. I loved those stories and heard them over and over. When people referred to verses, I would know the context. I don't know that I ever became aware of a structure, but I became aware of a voice and the beautiful use of language. I would notice, not intellectually, but internally, how language affects you and how it can express something in a certain way that moves into the body and hits you there." She smiles and places her hand over her heart. "I loved the sounds in the King James Version, and I can't imagine not having that music in my head.

"When I first read Proust and Robert Penn Warren I noticed that their language bore into the body, too, and I wanted to be able to write like that. There are so many places in the Bible that are affecting in that way. You understand it not so much with your head, you understand it in other ways. I was struck by that realization early in my life."

Besides the reading and discussions, there was a lot of storytelling in the Cox household. "My mother was a wonderful storyteller, and she usually talked about humorous things that had happened to her during the day. My brothers were also fabulous storytellers, but Dad was mainly a listener. Sitting on the porch and telling stories at night— that was our entertainment. That's what we did instead of watching television."

There was another important figure in Cox's early life. Ozella Davis was a black woman who lived in the Barks household for 12 years. She became the principal caregiver for the first five years of Betsy's life.

"Ozella bathed me each night and mothered me during my first five years. When I think of her, my heart gets tight. She was a mother figure for me, but I sensed conflicting emotions from her. More than anything else, I remember her presence, being near her and walking beside her. Her hands felt strong and flat. Whenever she brushed my hair, though, I would scream because she pulled it, yanked it hard into a small knot on top of my head. I think maybe some of her anger came out in that gesture because my hair was the wrong color. It was blonde. I wasn't her own child and she couldn't be with her own children because she had to work at our house to support them. I don't think she had a husband, but she had a family. We didn't know the details of her life because she stayed very separate. Occasionally she walked me to the school's laundry where other black men and women worked. She had friends in the laundry, but some days as the talk grew brittle or mean, she quickly took me home. I felt safe with her, but I was also puzzled by the anger. She left one winter day without saying good-bye. We never knew the reason.

"I saw her only once after that. One day when I was in the seventh grade, my mother picked me up from school, and Ozella was sitting beside her in the front seat. I was happy to see her, but I didn't ask her why she had left our family so suddenly. I still don't know the answer."

With the beginning of mandatory school integration during the 1950's, the South began to face up to the racial inequities that had existed in the region for over 100 years. "I certainly noticed the difference in color when I was growing up," says Cox. "I also noticed that when people wanted to be social with a black person in those days, they did it behind buildings or someplace secret. There were two black men, brothers, who drove the Baylor bus and did a lot of work on the grounds. I really loved those men and I questioned the fact that they couldn't come into certain places or do certain things. At the time, I accepted it as the way things were, but I felt it wasn't fair. I guess with school integration I began to wake up to it a little bit. I was frightened, because it seemed to me that if people hadn't been able to do anything for a long time and then they could suddenly do it and everybody was mad at them, it felt dangerous. I remember my parents were concerned, too."

In the 1960's at the University of Mississippi, Betsy Cox discovered racial anger on an even larger scale. She had transferred from the University of Tennessee and had enrolled at the Ole Miss when James Meredith entered as the first black student and President Kennedy sent in the Federal troops. Cox had left Knoxville for Oxford, Mississippi, because she was about to marry her future husband, who was in pre-med at Ole Miss. "I remember smoke and bombs and guns," she says of that time. Soldiers marched Meredith from class to class and everyone seemed either angry or afraid, but Cox recalls that some students believed that most of the trouble was caused by people outside the university. "Most of the students I knew, most of my friends, didn't mind that the school was being integrated. I wanted Meredith to make it, but I was frightened because I didn't know what was going to break out.

"One night in Oxford, my dorm was filled with tear gas, and no one was allowed to leave. I heard gunshots outside my window. I slept that night on the floor with a towel on my face trying not to breathe in the fumes of gas. The next morning I left campus and returned after the National Guard was deployed. Troops stayed on campus my whole first semester."

Like so many southerners who had grown up feeling comfortable with the predictability and inequality of black and white relationships, Cox felt burdened by the sudden awareness her own contribution to the problem. "I remember making faint efforts at trying to speak to Meredith, to nod or smile. I felt ridiculous, but wanted him to know how I felt, how many of us felt.

"The South that I grew up in was a violent South. Yes, it was intolerant, but the North was intolerant, too, in those days. The difference was that violence in the South was out in the open and in the North it was hidden. It's still like that. Everything is more open in the South: our anger is more open, our intolerance is more open, our love is more open."

Violence was to become a prime ingredient in Cox's first stories, but those were not to be written until after she was 30. "I never thought about writing fiction until then. I was never encouraged to write, but I was encouraged to get married and have children. That was in the 1950's. So I did get married and I did have children and by then both my brothers had written books of poetry and I thought maybe I could do that, too. So I began writing poetry and I got a few poems published and then I went back to school in graduate studies at the University of North Carolina. I worked with Fred Chappell and got my MFA in poetry.

"While all that was going on, I decided that I wanted to write a story. And when I did, I felt as though I had moved into a natural slot. "Land of Goshen" was the first story I had ever written and it was published in *Fiction International.*"

It was also about this time that her marriage to college sweetheart James Cox, a thoracic surgeon, ended, and Cox then had to deal with the added constraint of being a single mother, so her fiction writing had to be squeezed in around her teaching schedule. Given that she had grown up in an extended family at Baylor and that she had by then experienced the breakup of her own marriage, she found herself writing about families and the violence that can exist within them.

"Family connections are profound, I think, since they are so full of tension and extremes of love and hate and searching for balance. In stories and in life, it seems that is true. One of the hardest things to learn in families is that we all have problems. I try to remember that people are harshest with those they trust most, because they know it's a safe place, and they can be anything they have to be."

In *The Ragged Way People Fall Out of Love,* Cox explores the feelings of all the members of the family as they struggle to deal with the disintegration of a marriage. In one scene, Molly, the mother, reacts to her son Joe's announcement that he might move in with his father:

> "Is that what you want, Joe?" Her question came out calm and deliberate. She felt hypnotized by her own voice. "Do you want to live over there?"
>
> "Sort of," he said. . . .
>
> Molly looked again and again for cause and effect. . . . Everything ran through her mind . . . how it is too late, implications of what can be lost. Molly wanted to lean back into a soft chair of things that could be expected, even predicted. . . . Everything was appalling, clenched. Molly sighed and moved into the sound of her sigh.

Cox's first published novel, *Familiar Ground,* was hailed in the *New York Times* as "a work of startling originality," and the *Washington Post* said, "Cox can use words like blunt instruments—they deliver a knockout blow. . . . We know we've glimpsed magic that we can't quite explain." But Beverly Lowery wrote that "the injuries are simply too numerous and too brutal for the structure of the novel to bear."

"It is true that there is usually violence in my books," Cox admits, not in a confessional manner, but as a matter of fact. "I usually have a scene or scenes of enormous violence. It seems the story is not real until its hidden human darkness is exposed. But with each book I hope I learn to integrate it a little more. I think that critic was right. There was a lot of violence in *Familiar Ground.*

"I want to make violence disturbing enough to be recognizable. Neitzsche says that only if we are aware of our penchant for violence can we choose not to behave in violent ways. Being aware of what we are capable of doing is a necessary first step. Violence is a regular part of people's lives. I was trying to write about a gentle man in an unexpectedly violent world."

Cox believes that there is something about the South that breeds violence. The social metamorphosis of the region definitely had its effects on her. "Yes, it affected my writing. I keep wanting to come back to the idea that in the South there are a lot of secrets, some of them unconscious. The lack of tolerance and openness creates tension, which makes the place ripe for storytelling."

Even though she now lives in Massachusetts with her second husband, C. Michael Curtis, senior editor at *The Atlantic Monthly,* Cox is still strongly connected to the South, and she still uses southern landscapes in her work, including her forthcoming novel *Night Talk*. She has never considered leaving the South permanently, she says. Each spring she returns to Durham to teach at Duke University, where she is a member of the English Department. "When I come back to North Carolina, I realize that I have missed the thick air and soft light and the sounds of cicadas all day. There is a certain light in the South, especially in April or May, that makes me feel at home. But I have discovered a light in Massachusetts, too, that is luminous right before sunset, very intense, and shadows sharp as a razor. But I am deeply a Southerner. I want to come back. Yes, I will come back. My husband grew up in the South, too.

"I'm real glad I moved out of the South, though, because I'm learning things about it that I don't think I could have learned if I hadn't left. What I notice most is the difference in the humor. In the South it is slow, not witty, and it doesn't always have a point to it, but it invites someone else to join in and add to the story, so instead of waiting for the point and laughing and getting it over with, the way they do up north, you just laugh all day."

Cox also misses the slower pace. "That's partly due to the extremes of hot weather and humidity. And there is one other thing: distractions. We like distractions in the South. To build stories and create complexity in the telling.

"Writing in the South is almost religious," she says. "I think it comes out of the ground. And it comes out of something a little more unconscious, something wise and intelligent without seeming intellectual. It is the way Southerners talk. If you listen, you will hear something said that is very intelligent, but it's not going to sound intellectual.

"The Old South had a lot of secrets and a lot of violence and that creates a fertile ground for stories. I guess the secrets and the violence are a little different now and a little more personal. I think blacks and whites can really be friends, but not without recognizing all our human foibles."

Cox believes that in the future southern literature will take an altogether new form, leaving behind old stereotypes and exploring new ground. "I think the new southern writing has become more urban. It might still have a strong sense of place, but it will probably be less regional and the race issue will become part of all southern writing now. But Southerners will never get away from writing about rural violence, and I don't think they will get away from talking about the light or the heat. A Southern style remains."

Cox is proud to be called a southern writer "because southern writers want to write about a place they know and love so they can say something larger. If someone calls you a southern writer, it sounds as though you have written only about the South, but what Faulkner wrote about was universal. The problem with that label is that one is assumed to be writing only about the South. Each writer hopes to write about something more than just region—one hopes to write about 'the heart's field.' Writing well about a specific place gives credence to some other place; and creating a character whose struggle is humanly realized allows the reader to recognize parts of himself.

"Sometimes when I talk about place, people think I mean a particular region. I hardly ever mean region, though region is always implicit in what I'm saying. You have to write about the place you know and feel strongly about, and for me, that is the South. Still, I always hope my stories would mean something to someone anywhere. I am of the South, but my stories are about families and violence and even though I set them in the place I know, I have a feeling that other families everywhere suffer the same. The family is important because it is a unit everyone has or wants to have or yearns for, and when you write about those relationships you are writing about what everyone experiences."

When Cox asked Richard Yates to help her with her first novel, she said, perhaps by way of apology, 'All I write about is family.'

"That," Yates replied, "is all there is to write about."

Although it may be a while before Cox returns permanently to the South, she will continue to write about southern themes and southern settings, keeping green and alive in her heart her own special piece of the southern landscape, her own special place.

Excerpt from *The Ragged Way People Fall Out of Love* :

If you saw Stringer's Ridge from the air, if you saw the town, you would see how the houses themselves formed a circle around a fragment of the French Broad River. Houses began to sprout two miles from the river, and forests made the whole town flush with new green. If you came nearer you would hear birds in abundant droves, dogwood buds large. Blunt, fat-bodied swifts moved around in ragged fashion and rumors of bluebirds were passed from house to house. People in Stringer's Ridge were interested in such things, and since the town was closed in on all sides by mountains, they had a conscious faith in themselves. They looked rested and powerless. They looked as though they were always teasing you. . . .

The mountains of North Carolina unraveled into open fields and mossy trees as she drove toward Savannah. It was a sunny afternoon. Molly could never paint the sunshine on a landscape. She never got right the brightness against the shadow. Once, she almost found the right pattern when she painted an iron gate. In her own mind it was the closest she had come, but Asa never took that one. . . .

The dogwoods this far south were in full bloom. They were in full bloom last year when her mother was sick, and she knew her father thought of this. Molly felt stabbed by the sight of Savannah in the distance—the fat trees, the moss, the swampy places. Everything here delighted in its own privacy.

BOOKS BY ELIZABETH COX:

Familiar Ground
The Ragged Way People Fall Out of Love
Night Talk

Photo by Fred Brown.

Photo courtesy of Allen Weir.

ALLEN WIER

"As soon as you come up with some definition of what southern writing is, a southern writer will come along and confound you with southern writing that doesn't seem to fit the definition."

Allen Wier spent the first five years of his life with one foot in Mexico and the other in Texas. From 1946, when he was born, to 1951, he and his mother George Ann followed his father Ralph back and forth across the border, their visits measured by the length of their tourist visas. When the visiting period—usually about three months—expired, mother and son had to return to San Antonio briefly before they could re-enter Mexico, and then the cycle would begin again.

Ralph Wier (pronounced wire) was in the wholesale flower business in Mexico, which was in those days a wilder and woollier place. What Allen Wier saw, felt and heard there during those formative years has colored his work ever since: bandits and revolutions, exotic birds, rare and vibrant flowers. Jungle ferns, idyllic gardens. Hungry children begging in front of splendid cathedrals. Mountain farmers planting corn in clouds. Mellifluous Spanish names.

Now writer-in-residence and Professor of English at The University of Tennessee in Knoxville, Wier has all the outward trappings of a Texan—boots, well worn jeans, and a loose, confident walk that smacks of wide-open spaces. If he were a cowboy he'd be called "Slim." His slow drawl and crooked smile reinforce the cowboy image, and the contemporary house where he lives in Knoxville with his artist wife Donnie and 10-year-old son Wesley is filled with southwestern art and artifacts. But when Wier steps into his classroom at The University of Tennessee, he is mainstream writer, mentor to graduates and undergraduates, and a highly inspirational teacher. Here is a man who truly loves his work, whether he is at home laboring on a massive novel about a big chunk of southwestern history or in his university classroom, transferring to his students his technical expertise and his unquenchable enthusiasm for storytelling.

Any fact or fiction is material for Wier's vast supply of stories—his past, his present, a newspaper article, a friend's casual anecdote, overheard conversations. The trick is in the retelling, the rearranging and the embellishment, until he somehow manages to make the story his own. In the telling, he wades in slowly, his dark eyes sparkling, his grin unfolding with obvious pleasure, and the listener is hooked just as surely as Wier is hooked, even if he has told the story a dozen times before.

How could Allen Wier have been anything other than a writer? Those early years in Mexico plunged him into a constantly evolving fairytale whose dreamlike fascination has played out time and again in his work, especially in his second novel, *Departing As Air.* Later, Wier's father moved his family to Louisiana, where the family actually spent more cumulative years than in

Texas, but to this day, it is those memories of Texas and Mexico that continue to stimulate Wier's imagination.

An only child, Wier was showered with love and attention. He remembers impromptu picnics, ferryboat rides, and carte blanche acceptance into the adult world of his parents.

"I was born in San Antonio," he recounts. "My dad was from the hill country town of Blanco, about 45 miles north of San Antonio. My mother was an orphan. Shortly after she was born, her mother died, and then her grandmother took her. When she was nine, while they were in Texas visiting her aunt, her grandmother died. Then her Texas aunt adopted her, so Mother thinks of herself as Texan, though she was born in Joplin, Missouri.

"She met Daddy at Southwest Texas State University in San Marcos, which was then Southwest Texas State Teacher's College. Lyndon Johnson had gone to school there and after he became President, it was renamed Southwest Texas, and a lot of nice buildings went up.

"Daddy mowed the college grass and drove a cattle truck part time—he'd back the truck up to a laundry window of the girls' dorm where Mama, with a robe over her clothes, would crawl out and climb on back. He'd coast down the hill, lights off, till they were out of sight and she'd get in the cab and go with him to get a hamburger and dance somewhere." Wier fictionalized the cattle truck dates of his parents in his third novel, *A Place for Outlaws.*

"After World War II, Daddy got work in the whole-sale flower business. He searched the Mexican flower-growing regions and even the jungles for varieties of flowers and ferns to import to Texas. His Mexican crew called him El Jefe, 'The Chief,' or El Lobo, 'The Wolf.'" So that his family could be with him, he rented an upstairs apartment from an affluent American widow in Mexico City who had been married to a Mexican. His business took him to flower plantations in the state of Vera Cruz and to villages such as Fortin de las Flores, which means Fortress of the Flowers.

"While Daddy was working in Mexico," recalls Wier, "he had a work permit arranged with a Mexican senator; I don't think it was entirely on the up and up, because he got a call one day telling him that there was some kind of revolution—a small coup—going on, and he had to leave the country right away. The senator was about to be deposed; Daddy's arrangement would no longer be valid.

"We had all kinds of great adventures. In those days there were bandits in Mexico and there were roads with holes in them as big as Jeeps. A driver would have to get out and chop cane beside the road to make enough space to drive around the hole."

Mexico was an exciting change from San Antonio, where home was a post-war subdivision in which all the houses were exactly alike. On their trips to Mexico, the family would travel at times by train and sometimes in their bullet-shaped green Studebaker. On the train, Allen and his mother slept on a Pullman car in an upper berth. Images of that train ride appear again and again in Wier's second novel, *Departing As Air.*

> South or north all trains run through Mexico, either down or up. A train so far down, so deep in jungle, Jessie hears leaves, huge and wet, slap the sides of the coach and the windows grow damp with fog and the windows grow dark beneath the shadows of flower

blossoms spread like the pink lips of ocelots and jaguars. A train so far up, so high up in mountains, she looks down through white clouds at green lines she only half believes are rows of corn and in the window she stares close-up into the dark, moving eye of the black zopilote, the scavenger of Mexico, flying no higher than Jessie, the shape of his wings and the long body of the train racing on the clouds below.

When they traveled by train, his mother would dress Allen in his Hopalong Cassidy cowboy outfit and cowboy boots. He also had a fringed, cowhide jacket and handmade, hand-tooled chaps, with the cow's hair on the outside. "My mother had taught me very good manners, so I would pull out people's chairs for them on the dining car. We met a lot of interesting people that way."

During those first five years, Wier's only playmate was the young son of a Mexican doctor who lived next door to the American widow. When his friend waved a red shirt from the upstairs window across the courtyard, that was a semaphore signal to meet in the garden. "These memories," says Wier, "are silent except for the cries of exotic birds the Mexican doctor kept in cages surrounding the patio where we shouted and whispered and laughed with our arms and hands. We played by the fish pond where lily pads bloomed and huge black goldfish and carp hung suspended in the water. We were surrounded by lush shrubs, bright flowers, and tall trees. Beyond the trees there was a high wall with sharp points of colored glass imbedded along the top to dissuade intruders. I've forgotten that Mexican boy's name, if I ever knew it, but I am still sweetly haunted by the memory of his face as it appears reflected in the fish pond."

Afternoons, while the his Mexican friend observed the custom of a long siesta, Wier's mother taught him to read, write, and count. "I recall the smell of chalk, letters on a small blackboard she set up on an easel, the scrape of the easel's three legs on tile. The letters I remember most are: C U T F L O W E R S."

With their son approaching school age, the Wiers returned permanently to the States, first to Texas and later to Louisiana, where Ralph Wier eventually left the flower business to become a salesman representing companies that sold stapling and fastening machines. "We shuttled back and forth between Louisiana and Texas," Wier recalls. "We lived in West Monroe and Shreveport. I went to high school in Shreveport, to college in Texas, back to Louisiana for my first graduate degree. We actually spent more years in Louisiana than in Texas. Our family still all lived in Texas. We regularly went back to Blanco to visit my father's mother.

"My grandfather on my daddy's side had been a kind of mythical figure in the family. He was a great storyteller and trickster who would go to great lengths to set up elaborate jokes. I grew up hearing how he would have spoiled me. I would have had a pony if he were alive, they told me. Or, they'd say, 'If Herb were alive, he'd spoil you rotten.' So I loved to look at photographs of the grandfather I never knew and daydream about riding my pony.

"The family actually had owned a big ranch when they first came to Texas. My great grandmother, Herb's mother, gave her three sons the options of keeping the ranch or selling it and splitting the proceeds three ways. They took the money, which amounted to about $5,000 or $10,000 each. This was land they had bought for maybe 50 cents an acre and sold for four dollars an acre. We used to drive by that property—which had not, incidentally, been in the family in my lifetime and not even in my daddy's lifetime—and I used to fantasize that if those brothers had not taken the money and if my Granddaddy Herb were still alive, I would be riding my pony on our ranch right then.

"That probably made me mythologize the place more than I would have if my granddaddy had lived," Wier says now. But visits back to Texas made him sharply aware of the importance of place, and from those visits he created a store of details from which he still draws today. His first novel, *Blanco,* the story of a Texas family in the 1950's, opens with an almost photographic image of the town:

Jordan West's Sinclair station was closed, the glassed-in office dark except for the dim glow of the coke machine and a fluorescent clock, blue on the back wall. The Bowling Alley Cafe on the other side of the square would be closed by midnight. No cafe, no filling station, nothing stayed open all night in Blanco. The Lone Star picture show was closed weeknights, Fridays too during football season. There was no newspaper, no hospital, no jail. Blanco was the only county in Texas without an oil well. The courthouse, built in 1886, was empty, an election in 1890 having moved the Blanco County Seat some fourteen miles north to Johnson City.

One downtown streetlight made the shadow of a highway sign on the sidewalk. A flashing yellow light strung across the highway, and ignored by truckers who barreled-ass through town all night long, turned a plate glass reflection of the empty courthouse building off and on. A windmill, looking like an oil derrick above the short trees, was locked still. There was no water running over the new Blanco River Dam. But a westerly breeze and dips in the highway where flood gauge posts measured spring flash floods, suggested motion.

"I think in a funny way your place chooses you," says Wier, "even if that is not where you have lived the most years. Texas is certainly the place I'm from culturally. I never felt I was from Louisiana; I always look West."

Wier was accustomed to moving back and forth, so it didn't bother him later that he grew up with a double dose of religion. His mother was Southern Baptist and his father was Methodist. The family solution was that he would go to Sunday school at the Baptist Church with his mother, and then join his father at the Methodist Church for the Sunday sermon. "I was raised pretty traditionally," he says. "Southern, fairly fundamental. My mother was an open-minded Southern Baptist. My daddy was a good man, but not the kind of good associated with religiosity. He was smart, sassy, and often profane; he lived with gusto. I grew up hearing the rhythms of his speech, experiencing the sensuous details of his storytelling.

"Both my parents respected the value of doubt. I was always encouraged to question things. In Mexico we attended Roman Catholic Mass and over Sunday dinner my daddy gave me sips of his beer and wisecracked about the priests' skirts while my mother asked me what I thought the services signified. When I complained that I couldn't understand Latin, she didn't give an inch. 'You aren't listening hard enough,' she said. The next time we went to Mass, I listened harder, but Latin did not miraculously enter my ears as English. But, there in the hush of the cathedral, with the music of the Latin chant and shadows cast by votive candles, for the first time in my life I understood what it meant to be moved not by the thing said, but by the way of saying. As a writer, I acknowledge that daily.

"We read the Bible a lot, the King James Version, but my parents were not at all rigid.

"They didn't interpret the Scriptures literally. They had wine occasionally, and they didn't see drinking as evil. My mother taught me how to dance when I was about 12. She thought a man who couldn't dance was pretty much useless.

"My dad was pretty typical of that era. He would read the paper and go to bed and my mother would stay up with me and we would read the Bible. We read the whole thing from front to back. We'd read a section and then talk about it. I loved it. We also had a big book called *Stories of the Bible* and another big book of Charles Dickens' works. We read from those from the time I was about four years old until I went to junior high school and began to read books of my own choosing."

The notion of becoming a writer didn't actually occur to Wier until he was a junior at Baylor University. At that time, he had still not declared a major, but was leaning toward philosophy. The war in Vietnam was going on, and he was worried about the draft. "All of my friends seemed to know what they were going to do. Some were going to law school and some were going to medical school and some were going into business and I felt desperate to know what I was going to do with my life. I thought vaguely about law school. Then a friend of mine at Baylor asked me if I had entered the contest in literary writing. 'You like telling stories,' he said. 'I just figured you'd write something for the contest.'

"And then a funny thing happened. My roommate and I rented a little rundown house near campus that we called The Hole. We were burglarized. "I wrote a story about going with the police detective to the house of the teenaged burglar to retrieve our stolen property." Then Wier wrote a second story, drawing on his summer job on the railroad. The stories won both first and second place in the Baylor literary contest. The judges said that Wier could have first place, but he couldn't win both. The stories were published in the campus literary magazine, *The Phoenix*.

"That was the first time I saw my stuff in print. Later, in graduate school, I revised the second place story, "Cops and Robbers", and the *Southern Review* bought it—the first work I ever had accepted for publication.

"Winning that contest stoked my ego. I thought maybe I could do this fiction writing. I liked it. I started hanging out in a place called Big Boy's Truck Stop in Waco where rodeo couples mingled with Baylor students. They had a jukebox, good hamburgers, and a waitress named Sudie who'd keep your cup filled with coffee and not charge you extra. So I'd go there and play Hank Williams and drink free coffee all night and fill up long, yellow legal tablets with the stuff I was writing.

"At that time, Baylor offered no creative writing classes, and in the four years I was at the university I never met or even saw a writer. Because I had graduated from a Louisiana high school, one of my professors wrote a letter recommending me for LSU's graduate English program. LSU wrote back to say they were developing a graduate program in creative writing and they were holding an assistantship for me. I had ten days to apply. It was either LSU or Vietnam. I fired off an application, and before I knew it I was back in Louisiana."

In Baton Rouge he met author David Madden, who'd just been hired to develop the writing program at the university. "It took years to get that program going. It didn't happen while I was there, which was another lucky break for me, since, as the only graduate student in fiction, I had a sort of tutorial with Madden as my teacher. Never have I learned as much about how to read, and therefore, how to write. For the first time, I understood how technique could be moving and exciting."

During the two years Wier spent in graduate school at LSU, the war in Vietnam was at its peak. Like many other young men of that era, Wier was deeply troubled by American involvement in Southeast Asia. At Baylor, he had protested the war. His decision to demonstrate caused the very first rift between him and his father, a World War II veteran who believed that no matter what the nation's motives, young men should serve their country. "Vietnam is the only thing that ever came between my daddy and me," says Wier. "Because I'm an only child, and because I had been with my parents constantly in Mexico, we were always really, really close. There had never been anything I could not talk to them about."

Except Vietnam.

"I remember walking around Waco on a blustery March night, smoking those little sweet cigars with wooden tips and feeling very melodramatic. Of course I was afraid of being wounded or killed, but I was also afraid I might be forced to kill someone. That kept haunting me. Could I kill another human? I was patriotic. I was taking philosophy and religion courses, reading a lot and

being influenced by what I read. After having been a
Southern Baptist all my life—I had been a prayer group
leader and I'd given the invocations at our high school
football games—I declared myself an atheist. About the
same time, I declared my major in philosophy and
bought a pipe in which I smoked a tobacco my daddy
said smelled like candy.

"At Baylor, it was easy to be a radical. I was one of
about six people who protested the war. All we did was
stand silently by the statue of Judge Baylor. We got spat
on by some students who walked by, and that was it. In
the years I was at Baylor that was about the extent of
any anti-war activity on campus. But at such a conserva-
tive school it was a pretty big deal.

"It was all pretty predictable, post-freshman identity
crisis kind of stuff. I liked to tell my folks when I was
home that I was a communist and an atheist, just to
shock them. My dad would say, 'Naw, you're not.' And,
of course, he was right.

"Finally I sat down and wrote my dad a long letter
on one of those yellow legal pads that I wrote fiction on.
It was a late-night, honest but naive letter. I wrote
because every time we actually talked about it, he'd get
emotional. He'd say, 'You've got a college degree,
you'll get some cushy desk job.'

"Well, I knew they were sending people with college degrees into combat and he just didn't realize how
different this was from the war he'd been in.

"I loved my country, but I believed America was in
Vietnam for financial reasons, primarily. I wanted to do
the right thing, whatever that was. I admired most of the
young men who had gone to Canada or Sweden, but I
didn't want to leave America and not be able to return,

and I didn't think I had the courage to face being thought of as a draft dodger. So I wrote the letter about Vietnam, telling him why I felt the war was wrong. A good while passed and I didn't hear from him. Instead, I got a letter from my mother saying that my father had received my letter and it meant a great deal to him. She said that she and my father loved me and whatever I did, they would support any decision I made.

"I was hurt that my father hadn't answered my letter personally. I hadn't told him not to show it to my Mother, but I had addressed it to him in a way that I never sent letters home.

"Things happened. I got a 1-Y medical deferment because a family doctor diagnosed gout, which I don't think was gout, because it was a pain that manifested itself in my neck. I think it was stress and fear about what I should do about the draft.

"I didn't get drafted. I didn't have to go to war. The deferment allowed me to go to graduate school and it meant we didn't have to deal with the Vietnam issue when I went home.

"A decade later, after Daddy died, I was helping my mother take some things to the funeral home. She handed me his wallet. In it was my 10-year-old letter, folded into a big, fat square. Mother said it had been there ever since I wrote it. Daddy had read it again not long before he died. She told me that he hadn't known how to respond to the letter. He'd been afraid he might say the wrong thing.

"Finally, I understood. Maybe I understand even better now that I have a son of my own."

Wier's story, *Things About to Disappear,* includes some of the details of his father's last days:

> After nine months of sickness, slipping away from us
> a little more every day, my daddy died. Finally the
> cancer got an artery, it burst, and he went out in a
> rush. We buried him out on a windy, limestone hill
> beneath a twisted live oak. It was a time of leaving,
> the tail end of a sad summer. He was gone, and I was
> going, leaving Texas again.

Wier had always depended heavily on his father's
advice. The summer between his freshman and sophomore years at college, he was working at a minimum
wage job in a sash and door factory, standing in one
place all day nailing the same parts together over and
over. At supper one evening, he described the mindless
nature of his summer job.

"If you have a complaint," his father said, "write the
President."

Allen Wier did exactly that. He wrote a letter to
Lyndon B. Johnson, who just happened to be a Texan
and whose parents just happened to have shared a
duplex with a Wier who'd been Sheriff of Blanco
County. Wier sent the letter to his grandmother and
asked her to mail it, thinking a Blanco postmark might
get the President's attention.

Whether the Blanco postmark did the trick or not, a
week later, Wier came home from work and his father
announced that the President had called. "Yeah, sure,"
Wier said, laughing. But during supper that evening, the
telephone rang and it was a presidential aide who told
Wier the President had arranged a job for him with the
National Park Service. He could go to either Yellow-
stone or the Grand Tetons, but he had to be on the job
the following Monday. It was then Wednesday. The next
few days were a blur of activity, getting his 1960 Mer-

cury Comet, bought with newspaper route money, ready for the trip across country and packing for a summer in Wyoming in the Tetons.

The job was clearing trees and constructing mountain trails. "We packed in supplies on mule trains; our camp was at 10,000 feet and we worked above it, cutting a horseback trail up through Paintbrush Canyon." That experience broadened Wier's horizons in several different ways. It was the first time he had been so far from home on his own and the first time he had spent time with people from such vastly different social and cultural backgrounds. The other laborers were mostly sons of diplomats and high-ranking government employees. Books of all kinds were traded back and forth that summer—Kant, Nietzsche, Marx, Descartes—and popular books that included all the James Bond novels. Only one other young man, a Catholic, professed to be a Christian, and that was an unusual situation for a Southern Baptist from Baylor to find himself in.

In those days, Wier was eager to leave the South. "When I was in high school in Shreveport, I had begun to be aware of political issues, especially segregation. The summer after Wyoming, I got involved in helping a black politician run for Congress, and my parents were worried because the police photographed us going to meetings in black churches. The ultra-conservative, white incumbent became alarmed and got out the vote. He was re-elected by a landslide. I wanted to leave the South; I had fallen for the myth that southerners are generally less educated, less enlightened, and more narrow-minded than people in other parts of America. I wanted to go live up north, where, I thought, people were more open-minded and exciting and intellectual and where there would be no racism or small-mindedness.

"Years later I took a teaching job at Carnegie-Mellon in Pittsburgh and my neighbor, a guy who worked for U.S. Steel, invited my wife and me over for dinner, and one of the first things he did was make a racial slur about a black quarterback who played for the Pittsburgh Steelers. How do you respond to something like that, except to realize that if bigotry were just geography, then we could just cut off a certain part of the country and be done with it.

"Experiences like that made me long to go come back to the South.

"In a way, coming back home after going away and living in other places and seeing that temporal distance as well as geographical distance, put things into perspective for me. Things seem a lot smaller when you go back and see them as an adult than when you are a kid and think they are so big.

"I wrote about the South when I was away from it. I think I looked at it more vividly, but I don't know if it was more objectively. It might have been even more subjectively, because it was a kind of homesickness, and writing about it was a way to go there. More and more, I really believe in the transforming power of the imagination. I used to believe in it metaphorically, but I tend now to believe in this power literally.

"There are probably more writers per square inch in the South than anywhere else on earth," Wier says. "It certainly seems to me that in the places I have lived in the South, people who are writing tend to come out of the woodwork. Southerners are often writing family histories or a history of a town or community, even hollows, and they seem to have a greater interest in preserving the past and maintaining the Southern sense of identity. In a southern town you might be a crazy person or behave badly, or be addicted to alcohol or drugs, but you belong: you are our crazy person or our drunk, so you're okay.

"I used to think that southerners were obsessed with the Civil War because they wanted to revise the history of a defeated people. Because I grew up in Texas, I heard stories about fighting Santa Anna at the Alamo or Quannah Parker and his Comanches at Adobe Walls. My heroes were always Indians and cowboys—Indians first, because they were stealthier and stronger and wilder. That we often imitate those we contemplate strikes me as one of the fiction writer's blessings."

In a novel Wier is presently finishing, there are dozens of characters he is eager to spend time with every day—Indians, Mexicans, cowboys, runaway soldiers, German immigrants. "I prefer writing novels to writing stories because I like knowing that over a long period of time, every day, I can return to again and again to a certain place, the same characters."

Whether Wier has created those characters or whether his characters have created Wier is a moot point. And whether he is southern or southwestern is also a moot point. "As soon as you come up with some definition of what southern writing is, a southern writer will come along and confound you with southern writing that doesn't seem to fit the definition," he says.

"A friend told me recently that it is the southerner's absolute belief in original sin that sets him apart. When I was a kid and my father barbecued beef brisket, I stared at the coals and tried to imagine Hell. Now that

I'm older, I've seen the Devil more than once. I acknowledge a fallen world that contains unspeakable evil and the daily suffering of innocents. When I bathe my son, bump a soft bar of soap down his bent back as he leans over giggling in the tub, I feel beneath my fingers the fragility and vulnerability of his spine, and sometimes I remember running shirtless with my Mexican playmate in that Edenic garden where not even flies were allowed. The Scriptures remind us that God causes His sun to rise on the bad as well as the good, and sends down rain to fall on the upright and the wicked alike, and now that revelation reassures me.

"Writers are people who love to make things out of words. They are the lovers and namers of the world. As long as the act of writing brings pleasure, a writer should continue to write, even if he has no readers."

That has never been a problem for Wier, who has been compared to Sherwood Anderson, Robert Penn Warren, William Goyen, Wright Morris and the western writer Larry McMurtry.

In the meantime, his stories continue to absorb us and his characters to involve us because it is so easy to see ourselves through their lives, like June and Cage in *Blanco:* "They sat, listening to the sound of their own quiet sipping and swallowing, the refrigerator motor, the steady fall of rain."

That's Allen Wier the writer talking, embellishing, refining, elaborating on real life. He's there in that scene with us, but he's creating it in such a subtle and practiced way that we don't realize his presence, only the transforming power of his imagination.

Excerpt from a novel-in-progress:

From the Thurston wagon a deep, explosive report was followed by a puff of white smoke—Mary firing Hiram's heavy Spencer rifle—and an Indian fell from his horse, gobbling, like a frenzied, wild turkey. Dorsey scrabbled up the grassy bowl. Red dust was the sky. Grit on her tongue, smell of horse dung and sweat. Yee-yee-yee, a shriek male and female at once, falsetto yet guttural, a voice out of bad dreams. And other nightmare voices: Mary Thurston screaming no forever—no, no, no, no. Little Lucy and baby James wailing. And a loud growl close by. Dorsey's throat burned, and she realized the growl came through her own, clenched teeth.

Grass rushed up to her, earth hit her forehead, breasts, knees. Nose and chin and stomach slapped hard ground and heat flashed from her insides out to her skin. Mouth full of grass and dirt. She lay on her stomach and a heavy warmth dropped over her like a shadow. Had she eaten dirt before? The taste put the farm in Indiana behind her closed eyes. Indiana—why had she never pondered it—contained the word, Indian. Burying her face in the grass made the world not so bright, not so hot, not so loud. Was she asleep? That's what this felt like. She was sleeping and this was a nightmare she was dreaming. Or, the Indians were real, but they had killed her and the dream she was having was death. Dirt thickened Dorsey's spit on her tongue, mud cooled her gums and lips. She chewed, once, a satisfying grit against her teeth. Firm fingers sank into her arms and pulled her from the cool earth, rolled her over into bright sun and piercing screams. Alive, she opened her eyes, squeezed them shut, blinked away stinging dust and bits of grass.

Straddling her, his knees pinning her arms, a warrior not much older than Dorsey stared down at her. She'd never been this close to an Indian. Sweat and war paint made black rivers through powdery shapes of dust on his skin. He said something like "Why are peaches." Dorsey's throat knotted. She tried to speak; a kind of quack came out of her nose. He thrust his flat palm at her mouth, signaling her to be quiet. Around the edges of Dorsey's eyes bright shards of bone whiteness fell like hail from red storm clouds of dust, horse nostrils black and round as shotgun barrels snorted fire and smoke as the spuming beasts lunged from the earth, but focused in the still, silent center of her seeing was only this one, dark thing—this boy.

BOOKS BY ALLEN WIER:

A Place for Outlaws
Departing as Air
Blanco
Things About to Disappear

Photo by Dennie Wier.

Photo courtesy of Elizabeth Spencer.

ELIZABETH SPENCER

"If you live in a place 'till you're six, you belong to it."

A lthough she has lived for long periods in Italy and Canada, Elizabeth Spencer belongs unmistakably to the American South. As a frail and introspective child, she lived on the lip of the Mississippi Delta and developed an acute understanding of the southerner's strong sense of history and allegiance to family and land. Throughout a career that has spanned more than 50 years, she has side-stepped stereotypes to portray her characters with a dignity that makes her work universal but still decidedly southern.

These days Spencer is back where she belongs— at home in the South, having returned from Canada to Chapel Hill in 1986 for a part-time professorship of creative writing at the University of North Carolina.

On the outside, Spencer's house in Chapel Hill is unassuming, but inside are visible signs of a genteel life lived in a meditative atmosphere that she claims is spawned by some mysterious element in the southern climate. Amid fine antiques in her comfortable living room is a shelf full of first editions of Spencer's work, printed in both English and Italian. She sits gracefully in a comfortable chair, dressed in slim slacks and a silky printed blouse. Her manners are exemplary of a woman reared to be the consummate southern lady, although her enviable posture is part dignified bearing, part pure determination and backbone. In short, there is more to Elizabeth Spencer than meets the eye.

In Spencer's speech, in the way she moves, you sense that slower pace so typical of the South—a pace the author attributes to the heat. Despite her prodigious travels, hers is still a distinctly southern accent. "If you live in a place 'till you're six," she says, "you belong to it."

When Spencer moved to Canada in 1956 after marrying John Rusher, a British businessman she met in Italy, she worried at first about being so far away from her birthplace. If she was going to write about the South, she thought, she should be living there. Eventually, though, she realized that her southernness was an integral part of her personality, never to be excised. "The Southerner has a certain mentality," she says in *Contemporary Authors,* "especially Southern women— you can no more change a Southern woman than you can a French woman; they're always going to be French no matter what you do. . . . It seemed to me that there wasn't any need in sitting at home in the cotton field just to be Southern, that you could be Southern elsewhere, in Florence, or Paris, or anywhere you found yourself." Her assessment of the ingrained southern heritage has proved accurate: Critics have praised her ability to portray the South without exaggeration or caricature and to write with honesty about both its strengths and its shortcomings.

The more meditative pace Spencer attributes to the South is a rhythm to which she has moved throughout her life. From her girlhood, she has been introspective and contemplative, weighing events and relationships with a great deal of thought, perhaps because, growing up, she felt a sense of isolation, even within her own family. The complexities of family and community relationships soon became constant themes in her work, and her family life proved to be a laboratory for her later books.

Her father was a businessman she describes as "practical," with "hard sense," who later tried to discourage her writing. Spencer says she inherited her father's bad temper, and perhaps that is why she never had a close relationship with him. It was different with her mother, whom Spencer describes as playful and imaginative during her younger years. She fueled her daughter's sense of creativity by constantly reading to her—Dickens, Scott, mythology, the Bible, and she encouraged Spencer's early writing endeavors. But later, when Spencer began to deal with the race issue, her mother was less receptive. Spencer explains the ambivalence by saying that her mother could never adjust to "modern" writing by anybody she knew, especially her own daughter. In addition, she felt that her parents were embarrassed by some of the realistic aspects of her work. They objected to her candid treatment of the predicament of southern blacks in *The Voice at the Back Door.* They wanted her to give up writing, she said, and get married and have a family. Spencer speculates that they might have feared the loss of domination they had had over her when she was a child, a tendency she believes to be prevalent in southern families.

Her recurrent illnesses might also have contributed to her sense of isolation. "I was sickly as a child," Spencer says. "I had some kind of serious intestinal stuff, which they said was malaria, so they almost killed me with quinine before the illness was diagnosed as something else. And I must have had pneumonia, because when I was living in Canada and had to have x-rays for something else, they found a lot of scars on my lungs. It was damp and cold in Carrollton, Mississippi, in the winter, and I got more than my share of illnesses. I couldn't really keep up and I was not very good in sports, though I used to do tennis and horseback riding. My brother Luther is seven years older, and we would ride together on my uncle's plantation, but we never got along very well." Others who knew the family thought her older brother was affectionate and sometimes even adoring of his sister, but Spencer remembers it differently. "I always thought he was cold to me," she says.

Spencer's early emotional alienation made her something of a loner and perhaps contributed to her keen observations of the life around her: The strong sense of place she developed became one of the most powerful elements in her writing. "I grew up in a very small town," she says. "I think it was about 500 population. Our house was on the outskirts of town, with 40 acres that looked down over levels of farmland to the creek. Carrollton is actually an old hill town on the edge of the hills in the Delta. I remember once that the creek flooded, and my brother had to swim down into the fields to get the mules out. That was Big Sand Creek. Valley Hill was the place we thought was so dramatic. You would go down this long hill and suddenly there was the whole delta opening out in front of you.

"The house I lived in was not a farmhouse at all. People in Carrollton built very impressive houses. Our house was post-Civil War, but a lot of our neighbors had the best classical houses. We had somebody come in and plant cotton there in front of the house, and later on we had cattle. I used to keep horses, and we had our own chickens and sometimes hogs. I guess you could call it a farm, even though we thought of ourselves as living in town. The house was one story, kind of spread out with a big open front hallway and a gatewalk. One gable came out from the main part and there were window seats in the windows. A bedroom, a living room and a dining room were in the front, a kitchen in the back, and two bedrooms on the other end. We had a swing on the porch across the front of the house. I often dream about that house. I have used houses around Mississippi as settings because I think those old houses are full of a poetic or dramatic sense of something that has gone on in them. Allen Tate, the poet, said there were two southern art forms: one was home architecture and the other was literature. And I think he was right.

"In school people were always baiting us because we didn't have indoor bathrooms, but I think I had a terribly interesting childhood." Spencer remembers the best times as those spent on a plantation in Teoc owned by her uncle and his wife. Teoc was also the site of the local post office. "I had my horse down on the plantation," Spencer recalls, "and my uncle had to cover the grounds on horseback, so I would get my horse and ride with him. Sometimes we would ride 20 to 30 miles a day. My grandmother, who was a great devotee of Sir Walter Scott's novels, named the plantation Waverly, after Scott's novel, but nobody else called it that. It was just called Teoc."

From the beginning of Spencer's life, her mother strongly emphasized gentility, breeding and propriety. When it came time for church, Elizabeth was dressed up in fancy dresses, white socks and patent leather shoes, and in the winter she wore kid gloves. But at Teoc, she seemed to have absolute freedom. There, she wore overalls and a straw hat. On Saturdays, she worked in the plantation store for black tenants, selling shoes, sardines, snuff, and eggs. The tenants, she says fondly, were her great friends when she was a small girl. Some days she would go fishing with them, or climbing trees in the swamp. "I was all over the place," she recalls, "but of course when I got to be an adolescent, all of that was cut off. When you became a young lady, they didn't have the same attitude."

The tenants also inspired Spencer's love of ghost stories. "I believe in ghosts," Spencer insists. "I used to be told ghost stories all the time by black people when I was down at the plantation. They would tell you events that had happened that were just extraordinary—that they had seen dead people, for instance. But I don't think they told all that just for me: they would be swapping stories amongst each other and I would overhear. There was a ghost that hung around my hometown and I wrote a story about it called 'First Dark,' which is what we call the long twilight that we have in the Deep South."

At first Spencer automatically accepted the economic and social demarcations between blacks and whites, but as she grew older, she began to realize the enormous inequities. "I was a quarrelsome child," she says, "and I used to have long arguments with my parents because the Episcopal Church had a bench in the back where our house servants had to sit. Their answer to my argument was that the Negroes had their own church. It wasn't until I started writing my stories that I began to actively question the whole southern segregation arrangement. I had taken for granted that this was the way of life and people did what was expected of them. I believed what people told me when they said that Negroes were an inferior race and that we had the responsibility for looking after them. And then I went off to Italy on a Guggenheim in 1953 with a plan to write about an imaginary town with imaginary people, an examination of what might have happened between blacks and whites. It was *Voices at the Back Door.* When I came home with the manuscript of this novel two years later, all hell had cut loose about segregation, and I got in real hot water. So I never did go back to live in Carrollton. I visited a number of times to see my family and to do what I could for my mother and father, but I never really got back to live in the South until I came back to Chapel Hill." The censure she experienced only increased her determination to continue telling the truth about her beloved South.

As an example of the level of prejudice in Mississippi in those days, Spencer cites the episode in August 1955 involving Emmett Till, a 14-year-old black boy from Chicago who had come down to visit his grandmother in Money, Mississippi. He had been bragging about having a white girlfriend and white friends in Chicago, and then he allegedly whistled at a good-looking white woman outside a country store. His fatal beating and the eventual acquittal of his kidnappers was one of the catalysts for the Civil Rights Movement in the South in the mid-Fifties. "These things will go on forever being rehashed in the South because it was such a dramatic time," says Spencer, " a series of dramatic confrontations, deaths and killings. I think I developed myself in the course of writing *The Voice at the Back Door.* I was writing from memory, but all the voices came back to me and all the things that people had said all my life that I had never evaluated. I suddenly began to look at them and see what a sorry state things were in. One reason the book became a bestseller and was translated into five or six languages was that national interest was swinging toward the issue and I just happened to hit the convergence of the two."

Spencer digs far enough under the turf of the southern landscape to expose injustices that might often seem vaguely bothersome to her readers, sometimes shameful, even unanswerable. However, she refuses to be accountable for the actions of her characters. For example, in "The Business Venture," the reader might think the black man and white woman are going to have a love affair, but Spencer says, "I don't think they were lovers at all." And when she talks about *The Light in the Piazza,* she claims she really doesn't know whether the Italian father understands the true condition of the slightly retarded American girl his son is so eager to marry. In an interview with Irv Broughton, Spencer said, ". . . I don't know if he did or not. I couldn't tell that he had understood and I don't think he ever did." Neither, she says, does she know whether the marriage of Clara and Fabrizio will work out in the long run. Once her characters take form, Spencer imagines a continuing life for them beyond the end of her stories, but she lets them do as they please, even when she sees they are going to make mistakes. All she can do at that point, she says, is promise not to judge them. This kind of authorial tough love may be a reflection of events in Spencer's childhood, when she learned from family and community a series of lessons that steered her firmly toward independence. It is as if she has set things in motion in her stories and then lets that initial energy take the characters where it will. In fact, Spencer makes us think about her characters and their decisions long after we have turned the last page in a book or story, in the same way we worry about the futures of our children or our friends.

"Well, it's all grist for your mill," she says, "whatever your experience is. You can transform it into fiction, but you won't do so well if you write about things you don't know anything about. As soon as I learned to write, I began putting things down. This is a lifelong habit I fell into. I loved stories and before I could write I used to make up stories and tell them to myself. When I was about six I wrote a story set at the North Pole, of all places. It was about a child who was kidnapped from a plantation in Mississippi and taken to the North Pole. I gave it to my mother and father for Christmas. I think I got onto that idea by reading my brother's boys' books and adventure magazine stories about distant places."

The fairy tales her mother had read to her as a child were also influential in generating ideas for Spencer's later stories. "You take a plot thread, a configuration of people like a domineering mother, a daughter who has to stay there with her because she is in bad health. That could derive from the Princess and the Wicked Witch who is holding her captive. So then the Prince will come, you see, and that will be the young man who is an insurance salesman. So I used things like that to build a base for short stories. The structure of the stories, the configuration of characters, who dominates whom, who wants to get out, what's the predicament: those are good, lasting sort of approaches to life, and I used those things in a lot of stories. *The Light in the Piazza* was about a girl who had the handicap of a childhood injury, but then she got into a totally different environment. To me that was the story of the princess with the harelip who thought she was condemned never to attract anyone. It turned out the prince who loved her didn't even notice it."

Religion also played an important role in Spencer's writing because of her early exposure to the Bible. Although she became an Episcopalian when she married, Spencer grew up as a Presbyterian. "Oh my word," she says, laughing, "You can't believe the prohibitions. There was a great to-do when a cousin of mine who was the daughter of a Presbyterian minister wanted to go to a dance, and there was a huge family crisis when I started taking a cigarette every once in a while. Drinking liquor was strictly forbidden at home, but I think that if my father had taken a toddy occasionally, he might have lived a much more relaxed life."

For a long time, Spencer says, her family knelt down and had nightly prayers, and as a child she attended church and Sunday School four times on Sunday and went to Wednesday night prayer meeting. Even summer camp was church-related. And after that Spencer was sent to Belhaven College, a girls' school in Jackson, Mississippi, which, she says, "might as well have been a convent."

Spencer's community was also host to various revivals during the year while she was growing up. "They took turns," Spencer recalls. "One year it would be Methodist year, then Baptist year, then Presbyterian and Episcopalian. And when the preachers came, we invited them in and they would usually stay with us because my father was an elder in the church. Oh, I never got so tired of sermonizing in my life, but the good side of it was that I was brought up on the Bible."

Spencer also found a teacher in high school who encouraged her writing and introduced her to the work of Shakespeare, Poe, and Keats. That teacher, Miss Virginia Peacock, had studied at Vanderbilt and was so enthusiastic that she passed on her excitement about the classics to her students, especially Elizabeth Spencer. The learning was the most exciting part of high school, says Spencer, who felt slightly distanced from her classmates in a social sense. "I don't think I was very popular in high school because I was interested in books and poetry and talked a lot to my teachers and to older people in my family," she says. "But in the summer we all got together because we had a tennis court at our house and everybody would come and play tennis, and I was very happy about all that. But I think that the little bunch I grew up with weren't interested in me as a girl at all, and so I had to wait until I got older."

Those early conversations with older people whose stories she ingested primed Spencer for her ultimate calling as a writer. To this day she has a strong sense of history, because, since she was born in the 1920's, there were still lots of people alive who had either fought in or lived through the Civil War or remembered first-hand stories about it. Her paternal grandfather had fought at Gettysburg. "I was brought up around people my parents knew, and also my grandfather's friends, who had vivid memories of the Civil War. They talked about it a lot and there was a lot of 'Yankee hating' that went on.

The implication was that the South was better than the North and that northerners wanted to lord it over us, that they didn't understand that we had been vastly put upon both by the national government and by attitudes in the North. It was almost a religious attitude that southerners had about the South. Although that attitude has faded gradually, there is still a good bit of feeling about it, mostly among older people."

When Spencer heard stories about the war, she says, "I wasn't told that it was history, it was just things that had happened. But of course, history was what it was. It was a feeling of being connected to past events that were very real to you because they involved people you knew, or they involved your relatives.

"My mother's family were very prominent in the Army and Navy. They went to West Point and Annapolis. So my relatives were in foreign posts or in Washington a lot. An uncle of mine, a high-ranking Army officer, was married to a woman from South Carolina. She had a group of girls come from her hometown—I believe it was Spartanburg—to visit in Washington, and she called the White House and asked if Mrs. Hoover would see the girls for tea. And Mrs. Hoover said, 'Certainly. Bring them over.' Can you imagine? My uncle's wife called the teacher who was to bring the girls and said, 'You have been invited for tea at the White House,' and the teacher and the girls didn't want to go because they were Democrats. My uncle's wife said, 'Well you have got to go. I have arranged this.' So they did go, and Mrs. Hoover was perfectly charming to them, but they wouldn't talk to her because she was a Republican."

Wherever Elizabeth Spencer traveled, she felt a strong pull to return to the South. "People who take up life as expatriates lose something," she says. "Americans abroad who lose touch with their native soil are just not as fully based as people who hold onto their own nationalities. You always think that something is missing in some way." When she went to Italy after the sale of her first novel and went back later with the financial help of a Guggenheim, she felt compelled to return home to the South, even though she was in love with John Rusher, who remained in Europe when she left. "But when I got home I ran into a wall of opposition to everything I said, did, wrote. Anything. My father was dead set on my quitting being a writer. He had quite a bit of money by then and he would promise me money, but it was always contingent on my not following my work. So I took what little money I had and left to go up to New York and get a contract on a book, and when I did get a very good contract, and things were so bad for me at home, I just went back to Italy. After John and I moved to Montreal, Louis Rubin was extraordinarily hospitable in getting invitations for me to come South. Each time I got a chance to go back for anything, I would take it, so we moved back to Chapel Hill in 1986, but I never left the South with the sense that I couldn't come back or felt myself in exile. I just felt that my immediate home situation was too unpleasant.

"My father was a dominant person and took an almost tyrannical role, so I always just assumed that if you had a story to tell, it would have to be about a man. For him women were expected to have children and a house and to be there for him and I grew up thinking that in my society they (males) were the important people.

"And then I began to evaluate that theory, just as I did the segregation thing. I gradually began to develop very central, stronger women characters. I don't think of any of my books as being autobiographical, but it must be that my approach toward stronger women was developing through that element, and finally I got to very strong women like Julia in "The Snare" and the mother in *The Light in the Piazza,* who developed a great deal of strength in solving her problems. You can bring your characters to a certain point where a realization makes them able to handle whatever is wrong. Henry James does that. And that's the point where you should end the story. I don't think you should end like a Shakespearian play with everyone stretched out dead on the stage. I don't think you should end with a marriage or a divorce. You should end when the character has the hold card and sees it clearly. Then the character can act, and she does. Or is defeated. There is a lot in common between southern writing and the English novel—Jane Austin, say—the whole emphasis on family and marriage and money and houses and how you do things, whom you talk about, what your family relationships are. I think that is a very southern vein that continues on down to people like Eudora Welty and Katherine Anne Porter. Willa Cather's novels and George Eliot's novels also take place in small communities."

In the preface to *Self and the Community in the Fiction of Elizabeth Spencer* (Louisiana State University Press, 1994, edited by Terry Roberts), Spencer says, "This idea . . . of 'community' is a kind of ancient theme . . . . The whole sort of mystical issue of just who your brothers and sisters really are. It occurs over and over again in religious writing. All the central characters in my stories do seem to have that problem—finding out where they belong . . . and who they belong with."

Roberts writes about Spencer's 'southernness" in the conclusion to that volume: "Her first three novels caused critics to label her a traditional southern novelist in the grand tradition of the Southern Renascence. After 1960, however, she evolved into quite a different sort of 'southern' writer and did so in a way undetected by most of her critics. I believe that by virtue of her consistent concern with the dynamics of community she should be read as 'southern' even when her setting is Italy or Canada. No matter where the story is set, her primary concern is that quintessentially southern one— the individual caught in the communal web."

Modern southern writers have always had to compete with the benchmark of Faulkner's work. Spencer notes that a great deal of tension has always existed between Mississippi and the modern culture, and Faulkner was the first to articulate it. So everything that has come afterward has been evaluated in comparison to Faulkner. "It's what Walker Percy said," Spencer says. "The thing is, you can't get rid of Faulkner. Every time you turn around, there he is, but certainly that feeling has less influence on me now because so much of my life was filled with impressions and people that I met elsewhere, so the whole southern framework that he concocted, the fall of the southern aristocracy, the rise of the Snopeses, had little effect on me. I had been away for a while and couldn't think about life in those terms. There are some very interesting things coming out now about how southern writers like Robert Penn Warren, who lived away from the South, or Jim Dickey, who lived within it, remained southern but they didn't see life in a southern framework in the sense that Faulkner created the whole pseudo-history, a myth of the South.

So even though they weren't into the southern mythology, they still recognized the southerner and our feelings. I think that is what happened with me. My feelings are still very southern, but I'm not into the southern myth as such."

At 77 and just coming into a her own second renaissance of sorts, Spencer has a memoir coming out with Random House in the fall of 1997, "and," she adds, "I have two short novels, but I don't know if I'll ever develop them and bring them out." She hesitates and glances out the window, then says, "Sometimes I think I have written enough." But then, with a sudden light in her eyes that lets you know she has not written nearly enough to satisfy Elizabeth Spencer, she smiles and says, "But I suppose it is a lifelong habit. I love the novella form . . . ."

In a *New Yorker* article about her early novels, Brendan Gill described Spencer's work as giving off "the characteristic ghostly phosphorescence of something (slavery? The plantation system? The War between the States?) that went bad down there a long time ago and that threatens to go on flickering through the swamps and bayous till Kingdom come."

To outsiders, the country "down there" remains somewhat exotic, and why not? It has crocodiles, hasn't it? It has armadillos and deadly serpents that are sometimes handled in worship services at isolated rural churches. And though it has been altered by time and the inevitable march of progress, it is still a place with incredible inequities of race, class, and temperature. The same intrepid heat and humidity that coax forth luxurious flowers with pungent perfumes also sharpen the senses to that special sense of place for which south-

ern literature is famous. And as tightly as some southerners try to hold onto the old traditions, the Deep South
familiar to people born in the first half of the century is
rapidly eroding. Thus, those born elsewhere will have to
be transported to the country "down there" by writers
like Elizabeth Spencer, whose lifelong habit of writing
stories about her region has again and again invited outsiders to experience the "ghostly phosphorescence" that
"threatens to go on flickering through the swamps and
bayous till Kingdom come."

Excerpt from *The Light in the Piazza:*

At the wedding Margaret Johnson sat quietly while a
dream unfolded before her. She watched closely and
missed nothing.

She saw Clara emerge like a fresh flower out of
the antique smell of candle smoke, incense and damp
stone, and advance in white Venetian lace with so deep
a look shadowing out the hollow of her cheek, she
might have stood double for a Botticelli. As for
Fabrizio, he who had such a gift for appearing did not
fail them. His beauty was outshone only by his outrageous pride in himself; he saw to it that everybody
saw him well. Like an angel appearing in a painting,
he seemed to face outward to say, This is what I look
like, see? But his innocence protected him like magic.

Clara lifted her veil like a good girl exactly when
she had been told to. Fabrizio looked at her and love
sprang up in his face. The priest went on intoning,
and since it was twelve o'clock all the bells from over
the river and nearby began to ring at slightly different
intervals—the deep-throated ones and the sweet ones,
muffled and clear—one could hear them all.

The Signora Naccarelli had come into her own that day. She obviously believed that she had had difficulties to overcome in bringing about this union, but having gotten the proper heavenly parties well informed, she had brought everything into line. Her bosom had sometimes been known to heave and her eye to dim, but that day she was serene. She wore flowers and an enormous medallion of her dead mother outlined in pearls. that unlikely specimen, a middle-class Neapolitan, she now seemed both peasant and goddess. Her hair had never been more smoothly bound, and natural color touched her large cheeks. . . Smiling perpetually at no one, it was as though she had created them all.

Photo by Fred Brown.

WILLIE MORRIS

"My town is the place which shaped me into the creature I am now."

Willie Morris never really left the South. Forget that he became a big-league New York magazine editor, or that as a Rhodes Scholar he mingled metaphors with fellow intellectuals in Oxford, England. Forget that during his stint as editor of *Harper's Magazine* he befriended and promoted some of the nation's foremost thinkers and writers. Willie Morris, that good ol' boy from Mississippi who writes about his native state with tender prosody and vivid imagery, has remained a dyed-in-the-delta Mississippi product.

Morris confesses now that he felt like an exile during his New York years, and although he matured to middle age in the East, he eventually decided that a man had best be going back to where his strongest feelings lay. The South was in his very bones, and he felt compelled to write about it. "My mother always told me I was different," he says. "Some things are chosen for us when we are born."

Willie Morris lives in Jackson, Mississippi, not far from friend and neighbor Eudora Welty, who, he says "embodies what I feel about the South." His house sits back on an old, tree-lined street, the quiet, shady kind of street that says to southerners, "You're home now. This is the way it is supposed to be." Just inside his front door, where an unopened pile of letters is scattered beneath the mail slot, sits the beautiful old baby grand Steinway on which his mother, Marion, taught piano lessons and which Morris donated to the Yazoo City, Mississippi, Methodist Church when she died. The plaque on the side of the piano reads: "In memory of Marion Weaks Morris, 1904-1977. Organist of this church for 30 years. She taught hundreds of Yazoo's children on this piano."

Hundreds, yes, but not Willie Morris, who could not sit still long enough to practice. He was an adventurer who roamed in cemeteries with an eye for history and a curiosity about how life had unfolded before he was born. He relished those afternoons among the tombstones, picnicking on ham sandwiches and Nehi strawberry drinks.

In *North Toward Home,* he recalls, "On other days we would come and play until late afternoon, until the lightning bugs came out and the crickets started making their chirping noises. Or in broad daylight we would wander through the Negro graveyard nearby, a rundown, neglected area, fierce with weeds and insects, joined together by a rutted dirt road that ran interminably up another forlorn hill."

Morris has curly brown hair and rosy cheeks and a cherubic face that becomes even more angelic when he talks about his growing-up years in Yazoo City. His, he claims, was a storybook childhood whose details have been recorded not only in his own books but in a television special. "There was something in the very atmosphere of a small town in the Deep South," writes Morris in *North Toward Home,* "something spooked-up and romantic, which did extravagant things to the imagination of its bright and resourceful boys. It had something to do with long and heavy afternoons with nothing doing, with rich slow evenings when the crickets and the frogs scratched their legs and made delta music, with plain boredom, perhaps with an inherited tradition of contriving elaborate plots or one-shot practical jokes. I believe this hidden influence. . . had something to do with the Southern sense of fancy when one grew up in a place where more specific exercises in intellection—like reading books—were not accepted, one had to work his imagination out on something, and the less austere, the better. This quality would stay with one, in only slightly less exaggerated forms, even as a grown man,"

Born November 29, 1934, in Jackson, Mississippi, Morris is inextricably linked to his native land. Remove the man, and the stories fall apart. Remove the stories and the man disappears. Having grown up in the newly reconstructed South with all its continuing flaws and complexities, Willie Morris has written better than most about just what that means and what responsibilities it brings. The South is not easy turf, intellectually or physically. Its landscape, littered with the ghosts of literary giants, demands a standard of excellence based on the past performance of old, dead masters. Perhaps this phenomenon is responsible for the term "southern writer", an expression that some authors still find derogatory. It isn't that the South has had a lock on good writers, Morris believes, it just happens to have had a "gracious plenty" who have been awfully good at their craft. The river town of Greenville, Mississippi itself, he proudly cites, produced, among others, William Alexander Percy, Shelby Foote, Walker Percy, Ellen Douglas, David Cohn, and Beverly Lowery—a remarkable achievement, he says. "I don't know what a southern writer is. We aren't better at our game than others, I wouldn't say that. We've drawn from different sources, I think, and still do to this day. I consider myself an American writer who also happens to be southern." Morris says that small southern towns hold their people in a special way that is almost unexplainable, but it has something to do with loyalties, tradition and hardship as well as a kind of insulation and security, despite the racial trauma at its core, that may never again be replicated in American society.

Willie Morris, a sixth-generation Mississippian, grew up in a warm and nurturing environment in the kind of family where youngsters are free to wander and investigate the manifold mysteries of life. His first memory comes from very early childhood, when he was two or three years old. "I remember katydids," he says, "all over the place. I was born in Jackson and we moved to Yazoo City when I was an infant. That was the Depression. It must have taken him some time, but my daddy got the money to build a house, right down the street from where Aunt Tish lived. She wasn't my aunt really, but everyone called her Aunt Tish. We lived with her because she had a couple of extra rooms. Little old house right there on Grand Avenue. She is still a legend in Yazoo City. Anyway, I remember a porch swing breaking, an awful crying, and an old lady picking me up." For some reason, that is the very moment in his life that Willie Morris began, as he phrases it, "to take notice of the planet."

Morris is territorial about his past. Sometimes a memory or reverie will bring tears to his eyes. While viewing a Disney made-for-television film based on his book *Good Old Boy,* he leans forward eagerly to watch the boy in the film who plays Willie Morris as a child. "Watch what Willie does here," he says, and then he sits breathlessly, waiting to relive that innocent boyhood experience. "This really happened," he insists during the snake scene. "That snake should get an award as Best Supporting Moccasin." Again he assures you, "This is true. Everything in the book, *Good Old Boy* is true. Absolutely true." He grins, then adds, "But as Mark Twain once said, 'Sometimes you've got to lie to tell the truth.'"

Filming that story was like a trip back in time. "It was a very strange, eerie feeling," Morris says, "to watch some of these scenes, with people playing my mother and father, long dead, my grandmother, my grandfather. And here are the chums of my childhood being played by Hollywood actors and actresses. It brought back to me a bizarre rush of those vanished days. Hearing that dog bark with a southern accent. It was strange, but in a strange way gratifying. The film was deja vu of the most horrendous kind. Every time I return to Yazoo City, no matter where I have lived or where I have been, I come down that Broadway Hill, I am awash in memories. I know every tree, I have memories of things that happened on every street corner, every alleyway, every nook and cranny. I am suffused and overcome with memory."

Morris' memories are to him what artifacts and souvenirs are to others. He can take them out and review them at will. For example, when he talks about his

mother, his eyes dampen and he remembers how, on late
afternoons when her music students were gone and the
dusky evening hours were closing in, Marion would sit
at her piano and play, and upstairs in his room, Willie
would listen. "My mother was probably the finest piano
teacher in Mississippi," he says. "She was a graduate of
Millsaps and the Chicago Conservatory and was the
organist in the Methodist Church in Yazoo City for
years. When she died I gave her Steinway to the
Methodist Church in Yazoo City and when JoAnne (his
present wife) and I moved into this new house, I said,
'I'd sure love to get that Steinway back.' JoAnne got it
back from the Methodist Church, which proves there
are still Christians over there."

He laughs in a rat-a-tat fashion in his throat. No, he
says, Willie still does not play. He stares at the big
black piano as it gleams across the dining room and
hesitates, almost as if he can hear that music falling
softly back across the years. "Mama taught me, but she
kicked me out when I was about ten. She said, 'Get out
of here. Go play baseball.' Suddenly he smiles again. "I
was rather relieved."

Perhaps his mother, too, was relieved, because she
was a perfectionist. Morris recalls that when a student
played a piece badly, Marion would see the young
pianist through it patiently and then say, "Now, I'll play
your piece all the way through like Mr. Mozart would
want it played."

When Morris' mother was not initiating him into cultural pursuits, his father Rae threw softballs with Willie
and took him to ball games, but much of the time, he was
on his own, observing, recording, remembering. Many a
golden hour was passed at the noisy and crowded Dixie

Theater, watching the latest silver screen exploits of Roy Rogers and Lash Larue. World War II was at its peak, and Morris followed events through newspapers and war movies, even keeping a diary on crucial battles. Later, he was involved in a most human way in the nation's Korean War—he played taps for the returned bodies of dead youths he had known in his childhood.

"One day in the summer, an official in the local American Legion telephoned me. He told me he had heard I could play the trumpet . . . . I got my old silver trumpet and shined it up, and practiced taps with the first valve down. The next day the Legion official and I waited at the open grave for the funeral procession to wind up the hill of the town cemetery, and after the guns had been fired I played that mournful tune, nervous as I could be and wobbling seriously on the high-F. . . . The Legionnaires told me after that first funeral had broken up that it was far from being my last one. . . ."

But those lapses into good deeds and sentimentality were too awkward to explain to one's friends. The wild, mischievous side of Willie Morris was always battling with the intellectual side. And his public persona in those years was usually playing the 'good old boy.' He explains it all in *North Toward Home,* winner of the Houghton-Mifflin Literary Fellowship:

> If you were intelligent and made straight A's, got along fine with the teachers and occasionally studied your books, it was necessary that all this be performed, among the boys you 'ran around' with, with a certain casualness that verged on a kind of cynicism. So you would banter about grades as if they were of no account, curse the teachers, and develop a pose of indifference to ambition in all its forms. And you would speak the grammar of dirt-farmers and

Negroes, using aint's and reckless verb forms with such a natural instinct that the right ones would have sounded high-blown and phony, and pushing the country talk to such limits that making it as flamboyant as possible became an end in itself.

Morris' departure for the University of Texas in Austin was a turning point in his life. For the first time he was on his own, away from the protection of his family and the familiarity of his childhood turf. But in those sometimes lonely and confusing years in Austin, Willie Morris came of age, finding both a vocation and his future wife. He came to writing, though, in a roundabout way. One evening, he was invited to the apartment of a young graduate student. Before that fateful visit, Willie Morris had entertained the idea of being a sportswriter or a sports announcer. But when the wife of the student asked him about his future plans, his answer was a surprise even to himself. Inspired by the book-lined walls and the intellectual conversation, Morris replied, "I want to be a writer." He swears that is the first time he had really thought about it, and that very night he went straight from his friend's apartment to the library, vowing to read every important book ever written.

After graduating from the University of Texas with a degree in English in 1956, the boy from Jackson by way of Yazoo City took off to Oxford, England, on a Rhodes Scholarship. He returned to the South to edit the *Texas Observer* from 1960-62. After another year in Oxford to earn a master's degree, Morris became associate editor of *Harper's* Magazine in 1963. With his promotion to executive editor and then editor-in-chief, he transformed the periodical into one of the nation's foremost literary showcases, featuring the work of Norman Mailer, William Styron, Walker Percy, Robert Penn Warren, Bernard Malamud, James Dickey, and many other famous or soon-to-be famous writers. It was a world studded with celebrities and punctuated with long, lubricated lunches. Willie Morris, that good old boy from Mississippi, had come a long, long way from the upstart University of Texas freshman who, in an autobiographical essay assigned by his professor, wrote this sentence: "My dog Skip and I wandered the woods and swampland of our Mississippi home shooting rabbits and squirrels." In reply to which his professor penned the following comment: "Who was the better shot, you or the dog?"

Morris can laugh now about this event, which stung him sorely when it happened, though today he realizes that criticism is a vital part of education and that writers in particular are especially susceptible to criticism long after they have proved their worth.

Nowhere was this susceptibility more apparent than with the publication of Morris' *New York Days* (1993), which elicited a stream of both criticism and praise. *New York Days,* the sequel to *North Toward Home,* dealt with both the city and a broad swathe of America in the 1960's in the same personal and reflective style as its precursor. Morris called it by far the most difficult of his books to write. Most of the criticism came from people at *Harper's* who remembered the rapid rise and fall of the magazine differently from Morris. Laudatory comments included a rave page-one review by Elizabeth Hardwick in the *New York Times Book Review.*

But no one can deny that under his guidance, *Harper's* (which, ironically, is also the name of Morris' mother's ancestors) became a place where writers and journalists found an extraordinary home, a place where they could write freely about almost any subject. Morris' theory was that the fewer constraints he imposed upon a writer, the greater the finished product, and soon the prose in *Harper's* began to reflect the best intellectual thought of the nation.

After serving as the major-domo for some of America's finest literature for six years, Morris left the magazine under traumatic circumstances: his eleven-year marriage to Celia Ann Buchan fell apart at about the same time he was fighting with the bean counters who had taken over the magazine. Willie Morris' personal literary revolution had ended.

In 1980, Morris, looking around for a base, turned toward home and Mississippi, the delta with all its steaming mysteries and political skeletons, its sometimes turgid, gumbo-thick traditions. "If it is true that a writer's world is shaped by the experience of childhood and adolescence," he says in *Terrains of the Heart,* "then returning. . . gives him the primary pulses and shocks he cannot afford to lose."

Although Morris had already written copiously about his South, he resurrected himself. "My neighbor, Truman Capote, always said most Southerners come home sooner or later, even if in a box. I was rather reluctant to wait that long. Also, all my people are dead. I just felt it was time to be getting on back and I am glad I did."

"Getting on back," as he termed it, licking the wounds inflicted by his failed marriage to Celia, "a beauty queen with a Phi Beta Kappa key," and mourning the loss of his magazine, Morris realized that the return was both necessary and symbolic. The break-up of his marriage had stung Morris deeply, especially since it came in the midst of one earth-shaking event after another: the 1968 Democratic Convention in Chicago, the assassination of Bobby Kennedy, the election of Richard Milhous Nixon as president. To Morris it seemed as if the sky were falling.

But he was returning to a far different Southland than the one he had left behind as a Rhodes Scholar. He was coming home to a Mississippi that had struggled through the Civil Rights Movement, had been the scene of the murders of freedom riders and black activists. He brought home with him a keen eye and perception. Not only was he a Southerner with a soul, but he was also a native son with new-found vision for a land he loved.

When Byron De La Beckwith, the white supremacist who had shot Medgar Evers 31 years before, was retried in 1994 and ultimately convicted, Morris found some compelling words to express his feelings about his home and the South: "Beckwith's conviction by a Mississippi jury and his sentencing to life in prison could open up a new era in which unresolved racial murders of a generation ago might come to justice. It was not merely that justice was finally served, although that is a part, it is that this case suggests that prejudices can be examined and reversed, and that people and places can learn from their mistakes."

Attending the retrial of Beckwith in the Hinds County Courthouse where hung juries had set a killer free three decades earlier, Morris was moved by the irony, the plain sense of justice. "It was one of the most dramatic events I have ever seen as a writer, fraught for me with passion and consequence. I not so much witnessed it as felt it, for it evoked for me my own past as a seventh generation Mississippian with old serpentine emotion, strange and painful memory, the dark shadows of my past, and my people's."

Beckwith's retrial has forced Morris to re-examine the turmoil of the South in the '60s, most of which had surfaced while he was in New York. He wrote of his return in just about every story he penned, as if he were searching for his own misplaced soul and the soul of his beloved land. It was as if Willie Morris were sifting through the debris not only of his life, but of Mississippi and maybe even the entire South. Random House will publish his book, *The Ghosts of Medgar Evers* in January of 1998. In 1996 he collaborated with Hollywood director Rob Reiner on the movie "Ghosts of Mississippi," a story about Medgar Evers and his assassin.

"I was seized early by Thomas Wolfe," he says, "and today it is as if I am living my life right out of the pages of his novels. I was an American writer first, who happens to be a Southerner, who happens to have been born and raised in the South, the Deep South. A lot of my stuff reflects that, although I branch out a lot. I grew up in a small, deep Southern town before the advent of television. It was also before air conditioning. When you sit down on the front porch on hot summer nights and talk to the old people, you absorb their stories and their language.

"You were sitting out on the porch and they would tell you these stories, wonderfully vivid idiom. What they were really doing were giving us a way to see. The stories from the past—especially from my grandmother, made me feel that the past and the present are so intimately woven together. I have always been taken with that Faulkner phrase: 'The past is never dead. It's not even past.' He put that in his front matter to *Requiem for a Nun.*

"In growing up in a place like Yazoo City then, the town was right there before you. It was a town of about eight or nine thousand people, half black and half white. Everything was so accessible. It was like a story unfolding every day. You knew everyone and the gossip was florid. It was just all there for you. This was invaluable for a young person who would eventually become a writer. That really shaped me, I suppose."

His grandmother Mamie, the youngest in her family of 16 brothers and sisters, was born in 1878, two years after federal troops had left Mississippi. She was a prodigious storyteller. "My grandmother was the repository of all the stories that were handed down. Looking back on it, that whole relationship between the older people and the younger people, the stories on the porch, must have done something. It struck a cord. It also introduced me to the possibilities of words, of the language itself, which was indispensable."

Grandfather Percy was as much a friend as a grandfather. Morris fondly recalls going with him to the potato chip factory where the old man worked, cutting potatoes into thin slices and placing them in "prodigious black ovens." The two ate chips all day and drank water all night at home.

"He would do anything I wanted, from climbing fig trees to marching down the street beating a dime-store drum," he writes. As a boy, Morris was absolutely convinced that his grandfather would never die.

But there was also man's best friend. Dogs have always been supremely important to Willie Morris, and throughout his life he has had many favorites—Tony, Sam, Jimbo, Sonny and Duke. In fact, he will tell you that in his boyhood he never went more than six months without the friendship of a dog. But it was after the death of one of his greataunts that, for solace, Morris got a most unusual dog. Skip was a purebred English smooth-haired fox terrier. "We got him from a kennel up in Springfield, Missouri. I was an only child, but he was an only dog. He was my third, and I got him in the fourth grade. He was really important to me. He was so smart, he could drive a car." Morris memorialized Skip in the 1995 best-seller *My Dog Skip*.

During his teaching days at Ole Miss in the early '80s, Morris' best friend was Pete, a black Labrador retriever. Even though Pete was a Yankee dog—Morris had brought him back to Mississippi from Long Island—he called him "the last, best hope of the South."

When Pete died in 1984, the event so grieved Morris that he has said he will never own another dog. Today five cats have the run of his house. "Pete's death just about did me in. It was awful. That came out on NBC nightly news, on the Associated Press wire. They wouldn't let me bury him on the Ole Miss campus, though. I called the Mayor, John Leslie. I said, 'Mr. Mayor, Pete just died. He said, 'I know, I just heard it on Tom Brokaw.'

"I said, 'With your authority, can we bury him in the town cemetery?' He said, 'Damn right.' We had an Episcopal service. Pete is now buried in the cemetery up in Oxford, not too far from the Faulkners."

Morris looks off, as if searching the room for his old friend. "Someone recently stole his tombstone," he says finally, his voice wistful. "On the tombstone, it just said, "Pete, 1970-1984.""

Like the death of his dog Pete, Morris says there is something about the South that you never quite get beyond. It is a feeling that holds you between finger and thumb. And there are hundreds of places in the South that can grab you. Morris loves his native region with such passion that it would be hard to choose one favorite place.

"Oh, I've got quite a few. I love this town. I kind of agree with Walker Percy that for some writers it is important that you live in a certain proximity to principal landmarks of one's past. I was born here and spent all my summers here. I like Jackson a lot. I love cruising through the Delta."

There were many mysteries and myths in Yazoo City, some pernicious, some elevating. As a child, Willie Morris, like most Southerners, felt the irresistible pull of religion and before he turned twelve, he had been "saved," not once, but at least a dozen times and, at various times in church pageants, portrayed kings, wisemen, angels, shepherds, camel-drivers, Joseph, and, ultimately, Jesus. When revivals came to town, there would be a restless excitement in the air, but at age thirteen, Morris found himself disenchanted with religion. His fourth grade teacher, Miss Abbott, had introduced him to the Bible, but in an unusual way: Whenever her students misquoted an assigned verse, they were rapped on the knuckles with a twelve-inch ruler.

Yet that rhythm and those intonations were highly influential in Morris' style. As Eudora Welty says in *One Writer's Beginnings,* "How many of us, the South's writers-to-be of my generation, were blessed in one way or another, if not blessed alike, in not having gone deprived of the King James Version of the Bible. Its cadence entered into our ears and our memories for good. The evidence, or the ghost of it, lingers in all our books."

There was another religion of sorts that pulled hard at Willie Morris—sports. He loved baseball. Today, his family room wall is hung with photographs of sports heroes. Dominating the group is a large photo of Babe Ruth, given to him by former President George Bush. Morris excelled in baseball and basketball in high school, and his 1956 baseball team won the state championship.

The summer he was twelve, the local radio station started a baseball quiz program. "A razor blade company offered free blades and the station chipped in a dollar, all of which went to the first listener to telephone with the right answer to the day's baseball question. If there was no winner, the next day's pot would go up a dollar. At the end of the month they had to close down the program because I was winning all the money. It got so easy, in fact, that I stopped phoning in the answers some afternoons so that the pot could build up and make my winnings more spectacular. I netted about $25 and a ten-year supply of double-edged, smooth-contact razor blades before they gave up. One day, when the jackpot was a mere two dollars, the announcer tried to confuse me. 'Babe Ruth,' he said, 'hit sixty home runs in 1927 to set the major-league record. What man had the next highest total?' I telephoned and said, 'George Herman Ruth. He hit fifty-nine in another season.' My adversary, who had developed an acute dislike of me, said that was not the correct answer. He said it should have been Babe Ruth. This incident angered me, and I won for the next four days, just for the hell of it."

Also at the age of 12, Morris was a sports writer working for the Yazoo Herald and the radio station, WAZF. "I started with the Herald covering baseball," he recalls. "The first game I covered, I quoted Keats' 'Ode on a Grecian Urn.' I ran into the editor of the paper three or four days later. He told me, 'Willie, I really want you to cover some of these ball games for us, now, but next time would you provide the score?' Years later, Morris was asked to write the introduction to the Official Games and Souvenir Program at the 1996 Centennial Olympics.

Morris went from quoting Keats to talking with Robert Frost—not a bad transition. When he was a student at Oxford University in 1957, he was sent to pick up Robert Frost and take him to the Rhodes House to give a reading. "We were in a cab," he recalls. "Robert Frost was old then. He was always a curmudgeon. Brilliant poet. Beautiful poet. He said, 'Where are you from, boy?' I said, 'I'm from Mississippi.' He said, 'Hell, that's the worst state in the Union.' I was rather taken aback by that. I made some comment like, 'Yes, sir, but Mississippi has produced a lot of fine writers.'

"He said, 'Can't anyone down there read them.'

"Later that night, I was at a sherry party. Allen Tate was on a visiting professorship in my college at Oxford. He was standing there with Lord David Sussel, the historian. I walked up to them and told them what Robert Frost had said that morning about how nobody in Mississippi could read.

"Allen Tate had a very broad forehead and rather prominent eyes. His eyes lit up and he turned to Lord Sussel and he said, 'David, I have been trying to tell you for years, that's the reason the South has produced so many writers."

Morris smiles. "But I have discovered, having come back home to live, this one thing: It's an honorable profession to be a writer in Mississippi now. People come up to me in the grocery stores, restaurants and on the streets. Lots of kids, too. I have often suspected that this may be a kind of guilt reaction among Mississippians for the way they treated Faulkner in his prime when he was writing his greatest stuff. They considered him Count No Count. Then later when he started speaking out on Civil Rights, he'd get hate calls and hate letters. I think most of these Mississippi writers would agree with me on that, that it has kind of changed down here, very much so since I was a boy."

The issue of color is one that Southern writers have dealt with for years, with varying degrees of success, and it is a problem that has fascinated Willie Morris since his childhood. "Just take Mississippi," he tells you. "It doesn't have any big cities. You have a continuing, very complicated relationship between whites and blacks here. It is a state with the highest percentage of blacks in the United States.

"I go back to my hometown of Yazoo City, and with the exception of the big shopping malls, the four-lane highways and new subdivisions without sidewalks, physically the place has changed remarkably little. You go around to Main Street. It is exactly the way it was 50 years ago. On Main Street if it's changed at all physically, the only things that have changed on the structures are the names of the owners. But the race issue is much more subtle than it was. I would think that is true for the whole Southeast. One of our strengths in the relationship is that we have always said who and what we are. The old blatant racism that I grew up with no longer really exists here. It is a much more subtle phenomenon." In 1995, Morris proudly accepted the Richard Wright Award for Literary Excellence.

One of Morris' books was on the 1980's running sensation, Marcus Dupree, who went from the Mississippi county of Noshoba to the University of Oklahoma as one of the most sought-after running backs in U.S. football history. Dupree never fulfilled the promise, sustaining a severe injury that curtailed what everyone had believed was going to be a phenomenally successful career. Nevertheless, Morris believes that athletics has been the great expression of integration in the South. "Especially football, high school and college. We weren't going to school together in my youth, and I was just fascinated by the black high school football teams when I was growing up. They were called the Yazoo Black Panthers. They used the discarded uniforms of our high school.

"I would go over on Friday afternoon, sometimes with my dog. They would play in the black fairgrounds. I would carry the first-down markers, things like that. Great athletes. Yazoo City produced four NFL football players, all black.

"Living among the blacks had an impact on me. Oh, yes. The mystery of it when you are young. It was always there, always. It was very exciting and mysterious and I think that has affected every Southern writer.

"Race. That is the issue that runs through American life. We, as Southerners, should know more about it than anyone else, but I get saddened by it: We still haven't overcome it. The South has come along better than other parts of the country, but we still have a long way to go."

Willie Morris, the Mississippi boy once exiled to New York, sighs. "But I don't think anyone is listening to us."

Just as he thought his grandfather Percy would never die, Morris thought the South—his South—would never change. But, he says now, "A world I thought would never change has changed. I have said good-bye to the little boy inside of us all who will never grow up."

For Morris, remembering the Old South is, in a sense, a duty. *In Terrains of the Heart* he calls the burden of memory "terrible." There is, he says, the "urge to dramatize yourself about yourself, which is the beginning of at least part of the urge to create." But those memories and those childhood experiences have formed the core of Morris' character. ". . . My town," he says, "is the place which shaped me into the creature I am now."

Morris' summarization of his first 17 years in *North Toward Home* is worth quoting:

> I had moved easily among many kinds of people. I had seen something of cruelty and madness, and I had survived fundamentalist religion. My father had taught me the woods; from everyone I had love. The town in which I had grown up had yet to be touched by the great television culture, or by the hardening emotions and the defensive hostilities unloosed by the Supreme Court in 1954. Something was left, if but an oblique recollection: a Southern driftlessness, a closeness to the earth, a sense of time standing still, a lingering isolation from America's relentless currents of change and homogeneity. Something else also remained, some innocent and exposed quality that made possible, in the heart of a young and vulnerable boy, an allegiance and a love for a small,

inconsequential place. Only retrospect would tell me I was to take something of these things with me forever, through my maturing into my manhood. But then I could connect them, because I had yet to go beyond the most fundamental awareness of myself.

There are some lost parts of Willie Morris' life that are irreplaceable—his first marriage, the years at *Harper's,* his dogs Pete and Skip, his parents and good friends now dead and gone, grandmother Mamie's fried chicken and meringue pie, his grandfather Percy's model steamboats. But with his special talent for description and his rich store of memories, Willie Morris can reach back into the past and pull up his memories and breathe life into them again—for a while anyway, long enough to inspire the next story, the next reverie, a new link to the older South and America.

"People die and times change," Willie Morris says with a soft break in his voice. "But the memories do not die. They are forever."

Excerpt from *Terrains of the Heart:*

I often dwell on the homecomings I have made—the acutely physical sensations of returning from somewhere else to all those disparate places I have lived. To the town of my childhood—Yazoo—it was the precarious hills looming like a mountain range at the apex of that triangle known as the Mississippi Delta, the lights of the town twinkling down at night in a diaphanous fog. To the city of my college days—Austin—it was the twin eminences of the University Tower and the grand old State Capitol awash in light from very far away. To the citadel of my young adulthood—Oxford University—it was the pallid sunlight catching all in filigree the spires and cupolas of that medieval fortress on its estuary of the Thames. To the metropolis of my ambition—New York—it was the Manhattan skyline which seemed so forbidding, yet was at once so compact and close-at-hand. To the village of my gentlest seclusion—Bridgehampton—it was the Shinnecock Canal opening onto that other world of shingled houses, flat fields and dunes, and the blue Atlantic breakers.

It was in the East that I grew to middle-age. I cared for it, but it was not mine. I had lived nearly twenty years there, watching all the while my home ground from afar in its agonies, perceiving it across the distance, returning constantly on visits or assignments. The funerals kept apace, Abide With Me reverberating from the pipe-organs of the churches all too much, until one day I awoke to the comprehension that all my people were gone. As if in a dream, where every gesture is attenuated, it grew upon me that a man had best be coming back to where his strongest feelings lay. For there, then, after all of it, was the heart.

© James Patterson

Eudora Welty, left, with her mother and brothers.
Photo courtesy of Eudora Welty Collection, Mississippi Department of Archives and History.

EUDORA WELTY

"...The Southerner ... has got a character that does stem from his sense of place and of the significance of history, ... a knowledge of family stories, that sense of generations ...."

Eudora Welty, revered word-spinner of five novels and countless short stories, recalls the exact moment of her physical recognition of the word:

> At around six, perhaps, I was standing by myself in our front yard waiting for supper, just at that hour in a late summer day when the sun is already below the horizon and the risen full moon in the visible sky stops being chalky and begins to take on light. There comes the moment, and I saw it then, when the moon goes from flat to round. For the first time it met my eyes as a globe. The word "moon" came into my mouth as though fed to me out of a silver spoon. Held in my mouth the moon became a word.

From the very first of her stories, Welty's association with words has indeed seemed tactile. She has the magic ability to bend, shape, and mold them into connections the reader senses physically as well as intellectually. She strings words like pearls on waxed threads, sentences like soaring kites on sturdy filament. Whether it was her mother reading to her, or later, when she was able to read to herself, she claims there was never a line that she did not hear, and she heard it not in the voice of the storyteller or the voice in her own mind, but in what she calls the voice of the story or poem itself.

In *One Writer's Beginnings* she says that when she was only a toddler, she learned that her mother was willing to read to her at almost any time or place. "She'd read to me in the big bedroom in the mornings, when we were in her rocker together, . . . in the diningroom on winter afternoons in front of the coal fire, . . . and at night when I got in my own bed."

There were plenty of books to choose from: Mark Twain, Ring Lardner, encyclopedias and the Book of Knowledge, the ten-volume set of *Our Wonder World,* which contained fairy tales, Aesop's fables, and various myths and legends, *Alice in Wonderland, Tom Sawyer,* the Bible, Stoddard's *Lectures.* Eudora Welty's parents cherished books. In fact, her mother had once run back inside a burning house to save her prized collection of Dickens' works. When she was a child, those books were the bribe Chestina Andrews agreed to accept in exchange for cutting off her long, thick hair, which was so heavy, her father believed it would sap her strength and make her ill. She stayed up nights reading under her bed by candlelight, and her devotion to literature continued throughout her life. She read while baking—Eudora remembers books dusted with flour— she read while playing with her children, and she read intermittently while doing household chores.

Although Eudora's father, Christian Welty, was not much of a reader of fiction, he, like his wife, was determined that their children be exposed to as much literature as possible. The family kept a large collection of books in the living room, which they always referred to as the "library." When Eudora was nine years old, her mother took her into Jackson's Carnegie Library, which was just down the street from their house. Chestina Welty was one of the few people in town undaunted by the fiercely strict librarian, Mrs. Calloway. She introduced her daughter and informed Mrs. Calloway that Eudora had her permission to check out anything from the shelves, even the adult books, with the exception of *Elsie Dinsmore:* She was afraid that the section of the book in which Elsie, the heroine, faints at the piano bench after being forced by her father to practice too long, would influence Eudora to do the same. "You're too impressionable, dear," she told her.

Eudora was indeed impressionable. "Long before I wrote stories," she says, "I listened for stories." Her sense of drama sharpened her hunger for scenes, and her appetite for gossip had to be satisfied by listening to neighbors and playmates because her mother discouraged small talk and idle stories.

Among the important sources of language in Eudora Welty's life has been the King James Version of the Bible.

She also credits her teachers with contributing to her love of language and literature. The Jefferson Davis Grammar School was across the street from the Welty home, and when Eudora was five, her mother went over and asked the principal, Miss Duling, if she would let Eudora enter the first grade after Christmas.

"Oh, all right," said the intrepid Miss Duling. "Probably the best thing you could do with her." Eudora's anecdotes about her school days document an education that was both inspiring and exciting—Miss Duling's arrangement of a spelling match between the fourth grade and the state legislature (the fourth grade won); Miss Johnson dashing down the aisles of the classroom holding her black cape, upon which she had captured flakes from the first snowfall most of the southern-born children had ever seen; and, across the hall from Eudora's own fourth grade class, Mrs. McWillie, reading "The King of the Golden River" on rainy winter afternoons in a classroom that had turned dark because the school could not afford electric lights.

Her mother adamantly supported Eudora's desire to become a writer, but her father looked at it from a practical view, realizing that few writers had been able to support themselves through their work alone. Eudora tried jobs in which she could "use her imagination"—journalism, criticism and book reviewing, declaring herself "stupid" about office work. But her prolific outpouring of fiction and her intense energy and imagination eventually made possible a writing life.

Grit and determination characterized both the Weltys and the Cardens—Eudora's mother's family, who lived in West Virginia—even, Eudora says, before West Virginia became a state. Eudora's maternal great-grandmother, Eudora Ayres, daughter of a Huguenot mother and an affluent English father, married a poor young Virginian, William Carden. When they began their married life in the untamed mountains of West Virginia they had few possessions other than his leather-bound Latin dictionary and her father's wedding present of five slaves, whom they soon let go. During the Civil War, William was imprisoned on the suspicion of being a Confederate sympathizer and lost his eyesight during incarceration.

Her family's connection to that sort of history is what caused Eudora Welty to coin the term, "sense of place." It is that relationship with a town, a birthplace, and family that creates what she calls a "narrative sense of human destiny." Growing up in an insular atmosphere, she says, means that a person's entire life will be remembered, not just bits and pieces of it—"wedges," as she calls them. In the North, for example, you don't get that "sense of a continuous narrative line. You never see the full circle, but in the South, where people don't move about as much, even now, and where they once hardly moved at all, the pattern of life was always right there." Living in what she referred to as a subculture, she felt that as a southerner she was able to look at the main culture from outside. Perhaps that view of the South was enhanced by the fact that her father had come from Ohio and her mother from Virginia by way of West Virginia, and since her parents themselves had not grown up in the Deep South, their experiences helped her to distance herself to the vantage point of an outsider while drawing on her own life to provide the concrete details that make her sense of place so vivid. In fact, critics have found her European stories less convincing and enthralling than those with southern settings.

Eudora Welty still lives in her childhood home on Pine Street in Jackson, Mississippi. Her birthplace on North Congress Street, built in 1909, is to be restored to its original design in preparation for the construction of a three-acre Writers Center, of which the house, the centerpiece, will serve as a working retreat for writers from all over the world.

Eudora's work has also found a vast European audience. In January of 1996 she was awarded the French

Legion of Honor, France's highest civilian honor. She has traveled across Mississippi and the rest of the country, lived, worked and studied in New York and taught in England, but she returned to Jackson first because of family obligations and then because it was the perfect milieu for the vast repository of southern stories stored in her heart and soul. For a writer, the return to Mississippi from New York was a serendipitous journey. As a young writer starting her career in the overpowering shadow of Faulkner, Eudora not only established for herself a celebrated niche in southern writing, but she opened the door for other women writers to chronicle the philosophy of females in the Deep South.

Willie Morris is another writer who returned to his home state of Mississippi after a long stint in New York. Morris reveres his elders and basks in the traditions of the South. He honors the old southern connection to family and the past, and as a friend of Eudora Welty, he has written about her for the *Southern Living Magazine,* giving readers a rare glance inside the house at 1119 Pinehurst Street and a delightful insight into Eudora's personal life:

> She is one of the most gentle people I have ever known. She could easily have taken the role of the grand dame of American letters, but nothing would be farther from her quintessential composition. She is tenderly self-effacing. She is also very funny. She has vibrant eyes, very blue, a droll smile, and her white hair is short and curls around the top of her ears. Eudora is feeble now getting in and out of cars and going into restaurants or parties, but once settled she sits deeply in her chair and sparkles with tales and repartee.
>
> In our dinners around the town with a comrade or two her stories will be mesmerizing, moving here

and there in little circular sweeps: Greenwich Village
in the Prohibition years, or her fond memory of the
New York theatrical season when she was living
there in the Thirties, or the Dutch airmen training in
Jackson during the war, or mutual friends long
dead, or the dirt highways of Mississippi she trav-
elled with her parents as a girl.

[She has a] lovely, evocative Southern voice, quiet
and lilting, punctuated by laughter and the ebul-
lient retort, and all sorts of questions solicitously addressed to her companions. If the oral history of the
South lives in her written words, it flourishes also in
her spoken ones.

. . . She never married, and she lives alone now in the
house her father built in 1925. It is in a genteel section of town and was erected in the Tudor style of
those years, stucco and brick and beams. There are
two items on the front door: a Clinton-Gore bumper
sticker and a handwritten sign saying "No Auto-
graphs Please."

Inside, the house is spacious, comfortable, unpreten-
tious. . . . The kitchen down the hall looks out on a
deep green garden with a formal bench under a tall
oak tree. . . . Books are everywhere, of every size
and description, stacked on the floor in corners, on
tables and chairs, mountains of books. In a box on
the table is a medal recently presented her, the first
annual Richard Wright Literary Prize, with the
names of both writers inscribed on it. A substantial
new television set, given her by her niece, is not far
away, on which she ritualistically watches her favorite program every day, The Mac-Neil/Lehrer
Newshour. She remains much in touch with the
events of the contemporary world, often discussing
them with companions in her own wry and supple

way, and she is known too for her quiet involvement in civic and statewide affairs.

. . . . She has shown me the channel-changer on her new TV, and since she, like me, is not especially adept with mechanical things, her relatives had put small strands of adhesive tape next to the buttons for the five channels she gets. . . .

"What is a fax anyway?" she asks. I try to describe what a fax is. . ., chiding her that she may be the last American to know what a fax machine is.

"I still don't know," she says, "except what you told me today is more than I knew before. People will say 'do you believe in fax?' instead of 'do you believe in fairies?' They're about the same thing."

If anyone can make people believe in fairies, it is Eudora Welty, just as she made people believe her early novels and stories, many of which employed the literary structures of fairy tales and myths.

Reynolds Price, her long-time friend, has written of her: "In all of American fiction, she stands for me with her only peers—Melville, James, Hemingway and Faulkner—and among them, she is in some crucial respects the deepest, the most spacious, the most life-giving."

Excerpt from *The Collected Stories of Eudora Welty* ("At the Landing"):

The sun was going down when she went. The red eyes of the altheas were closing, and the lizards ran on the wall. The last lily buds hung green and glittering, pendulant in the heat. The crape-myrtle trees were beginning to fill with light for they drank the last of it every day, and gave off their white and flame in the evening that filled with the throb of cicadas.

There was an old mimosa closing in the ravine—the ancient fern, as old as life, the tree that shrank from the touch, grotesque in its tenderness. All nearness and darkness affected it, even clouds going by, but for Jenny that left it no tree ever gave such allurement of fragrance anywhere.

She looked behind her for the last time as she went down under the trees. As if were made of shells and pearls and treasures from the sea, the house glinted in the sunset, tinted with the drops of light that seemed to fall slowly through the vaguely stirring leaves. Tenderly as seaweed the long moss swayed. The chimney branched like coral in the upper blue.

Eudora Welty and author Richard Ford.
Photograph by Christine Wilson, Mississippi Department of Archives and History.

CREDITS